LIFE AFTER THE
NARCISSIST

A Guide to Recovery from Narcissistic Abuse,
Gaslighting, and Emotional Manipulation

Autumn B. Hayes

Cover design by Jennifer Stimson.

Before You Begin

To help you apply the concepts in this book, I've created a supplemental workbook, a free downloadable resource with key reflection prompts for each chapter.

Use it to:

- Reflect on your biggest insights
- Identify patterns you wish to change
- Choose small, daily actions that move you forward.

Scan the QR Code

Table of Contents

Introduction

I didn't leave because I wanted to. I left because I couldn't do it anymore.

Leaving any relationship is hard, but leaving a narcissist feels almost impossible. They don't just make you question the relationship— they make you question yourself. You start to believe you have a great life. And if it doesn't feel great, well... that must be your fault.

I spent years trying to fix that—therapy, meditation, more therapy. I even became a meditation teacher, thinking maybe the problem was me. Maybe it was my depression. Maybe I just hadn't accepted my life, and that's why I wasn't happy.

I kept asking myself, Why can't I settle into this? Why can't I just feel okay?

I'd go months without sharing how I felt with him because every time I did, I faced more gaslighting. Yet, when the emotions surfaced, they came with such despair that I felt like I was overreacting.

One night broke me open. Our child was young, and I finally said to my now ex-husband, "I can't do this. I can't handle it." His response? "Okay, I'm gonna get an apartment in the morning." No discussion. No emotion. Just cold detachment.

I spent that night on the couch, sobbing harder than ever. My body shook. My chest ached. Upstairs, he slept soundly, untouched by my pain—the man I'd spent a decade with, the man I was breaking over, was fast asleep.

By morning, I was begging him to stay. That's how deep the manipulation went. That's how much I'd been trained to doubt my own pain, my own needs, my own truth. I stayed another 13 years.

It wasn't until after the divorce that I read something that named what I'd lived: "If someone doesn't feel touched when the person they love is in pain... they don't truly love you." That sentence shattered me because it was true.

The irony is that I didn't realize I was in a narcissistic relationship until after I had already left. Maybe that's where you are now. You've left—but you're still trying to make sense of it all.

Let me be clear: If you're questioning your sanity, your worth, or your memories, you're not alone. What you're feeling is real. And yes, there is a way forward.

That's why I wrote this book—the guide I wish I'd had when I was lost, wondering why I still wasn't myself after I left.

Because leaving isn't the finish line. It's the starting point.

Chapter 1

Understanding Narcissistic Abuse

"The neighbors don't like you."

Five words. Simple words. Words my husband would drop into conversation as if he was telling me about the weather. He'd follow them with, "Nobody sees what a good person you are but me." At the time, these statements felt like love—as if he was the only one who truly saw me, who understood me.

I believed him.

And because I believed him, I changed. I stopped waving to the neighbors. I rushed from my car to my front door. I ducked into a different aisle at the grocery store if I spotted someone from our street. Each time I withdrew, each time I ran from a potential conversation, I proved him right—at least in my own mind.

Years passed before I understood what those five words really meant. They weren't protection. They weren't love. They were the first bricks in a wall that would slowly separate me from everyone else in my life. A wall I helped build, brick by brick, without even knowing it.

That's the thing about narcissistic abuse—it rarely starts with obvious cruelty. Instead, it begins with words wrapped in concern, statements coated in care. It starts so small you might miss it. By the time you notice the pattern, you're already caught in its web.

Understanding narcissistic abuse starts with recognizing these subtle shifts—the small ways in which we change ourselves to match someone else's story about who we are. My story started with five words about neighbors, but it grew into years of self-doubt and isolation. Your story might have started differently, but the patterns, once you know them, become clear as day. Let's uncover them together.

What Is Narcissism?

Narcissism is a pattern of behavior marked by an extreme need for admiration, a huge sense of self-importance, and a lack of empathy for others. At their core, a narcissist believes they are special, unique, and deserving of special treatment. They see themselves as superior to others, yet they paradoxically need constant praise and attention to maintain their self-image.

A narcissist shows their true nature through specific behaviors. They maintain an inflated sense of their own importance, demanding nonstop flattery and validation from those around them. They expect preferential treatment in every situation, from restaurant service to workplace rules. This sense of entitlement leads them to take advantage of others, using manipulation and control to get what they want. Despite appearing confident, they struggle with fragile self-esteem, which they mask through arrogant behavior. This combination makes it nearly impossible for them to maintain healthy relationships.

Narcissism appears in two main forms. The first is overt narcissism, which shows up as bold, attention-seeking behavior. These narcissists are easy to spot—they brag openly, demand admiration directly, and display their sense of superiority for all to see. Their entitlement is obvious in their words and actions.

The second type is covert narcissism, which operates more quietly but is just as destructive. These narcissists maintain their sense of superiority behind a mask of false humility. They might play the victim while manipulating others or tear people down with subtle jabs disguised as concern. Their demands for attention come wrapped in passive-aggressive behavior designed to make their victim feel a sense of guilt.

Both types of narcissists share the same core traits but express them differently. Understanding these patterns helps you make sense of confusing relationships and protect yourself from future harm. When you know what you're dealing with, you can start to see through the manipulation and recognize the truth of your experiences.

The Cycle

When you're caught in a relationship with a narcissist, you're not just dealing with random acts of cruelty—you're trapped in a predictable cycle. Think of it like a dance where your partner keeps changing the steps without telling you, but you're still expected to keep up. Let me break down this painful pattern.

It starts with what we call the idealization phase, when the narcissist puts you on a pedestal and showers you with attention, compliments, and promises. "You're different from everyone else," they say. "No one understands me like you do." They mirror your interests, your dreams, your values; you feel seen, understood, special. This phase hooks you in, makes you drop your guard, and builds a bond that becomes hard to break.

Devaluation comes next. The person who once praised you now finds fault in everything you do. The change might be sudden, or it might happen so gradually you barely notice. Small criticisms grow into constant put-downs. Your achievements become threats. Your feelings become inconvenient. "You're too sensitive," they say. "You're imagining things." You start questioning your memories, your judgment, your worth.

The third phase is the discard, where they pull away, become cold, or leave entirely. They might replace you with someone new or simply withdraw their attention and affection. The person who once couldn't live without you now acts as if you don't exist. This phase often hits hardest because it confirms your worst fears: that you weren't good enough, and that you somehow failed.

But the cycle doesn't end there. Just when you start to heal, they come back. This is called hoovering (named after the vacuum cleaner because they try to suck you back in). They might apologize, promise to change, or act like nothing happened. They know exactly what to say to reawaken your hope. "I've changed," they insist. "Things will be different this time." And because you remember how good things were in the beginning, you might believe them.

Then the cycle starts again. Each round chips away at your sense of self, your confidence, and your trust in your own judgment. Understanding this cycle doesn't make it hurt less, but it gives you power. When you can name what's happening, you can start to break free.

The Emotional and Psychological Impact

Narcissistic abuse leaves deep emotional scars that can affect every aspect of life. These impacts aren't character flaws or personal weaknesses; they're normal responses to abnormal treatment.

The abuse creates lasting trauma that can show up in unexpected ways. You might find yourself jumping at sudden noises, having nightmares, or feeling anxious when you hear a certain tone of voice. Small triggers—a text message, a song, even a familiar smell—can send you back to moments of fear or pain. These reactions stem from your brain's attempt to protect you from further harm.

The constant criticism and manipulation eat away at your sense of self. You might question your judgment, doubt your memories, or feel unworthy of love and respect. This damage to your self-esteem runs deep because narcissistic abuse targets your core identity. The abuser's voice becomes a constant critic in your head, making you second-guess every decision.

To survive this pain, many people develop ways to cope. Some throw themselves into work. Others might use food, alcohol, or endless distractions to numb their feelings. Some become people-pleasers, trying to earn love and approval from everyone around them. While these strategies might help in the short term, they often create new problems.

Trust becomes a major challenge. After being betrayed by someone who claimed to love you, opening up to others feels dangerous. You might find yourself watching for signs of manipulation in every new relationship, waiting for the other shoe to drop. This hypervigilance is exhausting, but it feels safer than risking another betrayal.

The good news is that these wounds can heal. Knowing where they come from is the first step toward recovery. With time, support, and the right tools, you can rebuild your sense of self and learn to trust again—starting with trusting yourself.

Why It's Hard to Leave

You can't immediately go cold turkey from a narcissistic relationship, and there are concrete reasons why breaking free is so challenging. Understanding these barriers is the first step toward overcoming them:

- **Trauma bonding:** A relationship with a narcissist creates a powerful psychological bond through repeated cycles of abuse mixed with intermittent rewards. When a narcissist switches between cruelty and kindness, it creates a dependency similar to addiction in their partner. Their brain begins to chase those rare moments of affection that follow periods of abuse, and this chemical response makes leaving feel physically and emotionally impossible.

- **Financial control:** Many narcissists maintain their power through financial control. They might restrict their partner's access to bank accounts, monitor their spending, or prevent them from working. If their partner isn't financially independent, leaving means facing potential poverty or homelessness. This economic abuse forces many people to stay in harmful situations purely out of survival.

- **Practical barriers:** Leaving involves complex logistics: finding housing, managing custody arrangements, securing important documents, and establishing independent finances. These practical challenges can become overwhelming, especially when a person is simultaneously dealing with emotional trauma.

- **Children and family ties:** When children are involved, leaving becomes more complicated. Many people stay to protect their children or because they worry about custody battles. The narcissist often uses their children as leverage, threatening to take them away or turn them against the other parent.

- **Professional and social standing:** Some people stay because leaving would affect their social status, professional relationships, or community standing. The narcissist might hold positions of power or influence that could impact the victim's career or reputation.

- **Fear of retaliation:** Narcissists often react to abandonment with rage, threats, or revenge. This creates a fear of retaliation—whether physical, legal, or social—that keeps many people trapped. The threat of what might happen can feel more manageable than facing the reality of leaving.

They say that knowledge is power, but with narcissistic abuse, knowledge is freedom. Understanding what you've experienced— the manipulation, the gaslighting, the slow erosion of self—doesn't erase the pain, but it does give it a name. It turns that confused fog of "maybe it was me" into a clear picture of what really happened. When you can name something, you can fight it. When you can see a pattern, you can break it.

Your story isn't over yet. In fact, recognizing narcissistic abuse for what it is marks the beginning of a new chapter—one where you hold the pen, write your own truth, and decide who gets to be part of your story.

Chapter 2

Acknowledging and Processing Your Experience

"That guy seems shady."

This casual comment from my husband followed the departure of my new business mentor. As a Brazilian, welcoming people into my home was part of my DNA, bringing laughter, warmth, and the energy of shared spaces. But, over time, those spaces grew quieter, emptier.

It wasn't just this one comment that emptied my home. It was the steady drip of criticism about everyone who entered our lives. A friend "talked too much." A client "only hired me out of pity." A repair person "overcharged." Each observation came wrapped in concern, each judgment delivered with a slight shake of the head.

At first, I defended people. I explained. I justified. But gradually, it became easier to avoid the tension. I stopped inviting friends over. I scheduled client meetings when he wasn't around. I shrank my world to avoid his disapproval. When you hear enough times that no one truly values you, that no one really likes you, that your success isn't real, you start to believe it.

Starting my own business should have been a moment of growth, of expansion, but do you know what he did on opening day? He went on a "business trip"—which was interesting, because he hardly ever had to travel. Each of my client interactions was another opportunity for him to plant seeds of doubt. "They're just here to help you. They feel sorry for you," he'd say, dismissing the transformations my clients achieved and the value I brought to their lives.

Why couldn't he see my worth? The answer was simple but painful: Acknowledging my success would mean admitting he was wrong about me. And narcissists are never wrong.

Accepting the Reality of the Abuse

Abuse is abuse. Yes, the word might sound dirty and cruel, and you might feel that it doesn't fit your situation. After all, you weren't hit. You weren't locked away. You were just slowly convinced that you were less than you are, that your perceptions were wrong, and that your feelings didn't matter. But emotional wounds cut just as deeply as physical ones—and sometimes deeper, because no one can see them bleeding.

Many of us resist calling it abuse. We search for softer words: "difficult relationship," "communication problems," "personality clashes." We tell ourselves we're being too sensitive, that relationships are supposed to be hard work, that nobody's perfect. This resistance to naming what happened to us is part of the abuse itself—we're trained to doubt our own experiences, minimize our pain, and make excuses for behavior that damages our spirit.

The first step toward healing isn't fighting the pain or hiding from it; it's facing the raw truth of what you've lived through. Only when we stop running from the word "abuse" can we begin to make sense of our experience and find our way back to ourselves.

Understanding Denial

It's a lot easier (and maybe even safer) to believe that you're the problem—that if you just tried harder, loved more, spoke differently, or changed yourself, things would get better. The mind plays tricks on us when faced with painful truths. It builds walls of "what-ifs" and "maybe-if-I's" to protect us from seeing what's really happening.

Denial is a psychological defense mechanism where we reject a reality that's too painful or threatening to accept. Our brains actively push away information that challenges our core beliefs or threatens our sense of safety. In narcissistic abuse, denial often shows up as minimizing the abuse, rationalizing the abuser's behavior, or taking the blame for their actions.

This defense mechanism develops for good reason. When we're in a situation we can't immediately escape, whether due to financial dependence, shared children, or other circumstances, denial helps us cope. It's like an emotional painkiller that lets us function in an impossible situation. But as with any painkiller, denial only masks the problem rather than solving it. The longer we stay in denial, the harder it becomes to recognize the reality of our situation and take steps to protect ourselves.

Facing Hard Truths

I used to think that if I could just explain things better, try harder, or be more patient, everything would change. This is one of the hardest truths to face: No amount of love, understanding, or effort on your part can change a narcissist's behavior. They aren't hurting you because they don't understand; they understand perfectly well. They choose their actions because those actions serve their needs.

Facing hard truths means allowing yourself to accept that the relationship you thought you had never existed. The person you loved was a carefully crafted image, designed to draw you in. The promises of change were never real. The moments of kindness were tools of manipulation. These truths hurt. They shake the foundation of memories you still hold dear.

When you stop believing you can fix the relationship, you can focus on yourself. When you stop taking responsibility for the narcissist's actions, you can start taking responsibility for your own healing. When you stop waiting for them to change, you can start changing your own life. This acceptance of the hard things is what eventually sets you free.

Coping With Acceptance

Joy can coexist with sadness, healing can coexist with hurt, and acceptance doesn't mean approval. Accepting what happened doesn't mean you excuse it or that it was okay. It means you stop fighting against the reality of your experience and start putting your energy into healing.

Acceptance comes in waves. Some days, you'll feel strong, clear-headed, and ready to move forward. Other days, old doubts might creep back in and you might question everything all over again. This isn't failure—it's part of healing. Each time you choose to face the truth instead of hiding from it, you grow stronger.

When you accept what happened, you take back your power. You stop trying to make sense of the senseless or find logic in the illogical. You can finally put down the heavy burden of trying to fix someone else and focus on rebuilding your own life. This is where true healing begins—not in forgetting or forgiving, but in accepting your experience as part of your story without letting it define your future.

Moving Toward Acceptance

Acceptance is a practice you build day by day:

- Start by noticing your thoughts without judging them. When you catch yourself making excuses for abuse or blaming yourself, pause. Don't fight these thoughts; just observe them.

- Write down your experiences. Put your memories on paper, exactly as you remember them—don't edit or soften what happened. Include how you felt in those moments, not just what happened. This creates a record that's harder to doubt when self-questioning creeps in.

- Talk about your experience with people who understand— whether that's a therapist, a support group, or trusted friends. Speaking your truth out loud makes it more real and breaks the isolation created by abuse.

- Notice the ways in which you've grown stronger through this experience. Maybe you've learned to trust your instincts, set boundaries, or speak up for yourself. These aren't just consolation prizes; they're also proof of your resilience.

- Feel your feelings without trying to fix them. Anger shows you where your boundaries were crossed, sadness honors what you've lost, while fear points to places that need healing. Each emotion has something to teach you about your experience and your needs.

Building Resilience

The heart is a remarkable organ, and not just because it keeps us alive. After every heartbreak, every wound, it keeps beating. It doesn't just survive; it grows stronger. This biological resilience reflects a deeper truth about human psychology and our capacity to recover from trauma.

In psychology, resilience means the ability to adapt to stress and adversity while maintaining mental and emotional stability. It's not a trait we're born with or without—it's a set of skills we can develop. The most resilient people share key characteristics: They maintain strong social connections, face their fears instead of avoiding them, and develop a realistic sense of control over their lives.

For survivors of narcissistic abuse, resilience takes on special significance because the prolonged exposure to manipulation and emotional trauma often damages our natural coping mechanisms. We might lose trust in our judgment, doubt our perceptions, or develop unhealthy survival strategies. To build resilience, we have to learn to trust ourselves again, teach ourselves how to develop healthy boundaries, and create new patterns of thinking and behaving.

Here's how to build resilience:

- **Support systems:** Building strong relationships creates a safety net for when you struggle. This means reconnecting with old friends, making new ones, joining support groups, or working with a therapist. Social support reduces isolation and provides different perspectives when self-doubt creeps in.

- **Self-trust:** Start small. Notice when your gut is telling you that something feels wrong. Write down your thoughts and feelings without questioning them. Practice making decisions without seeking approval from others. Each time you trust your judgment and survive the outcome, your self-trust grows stronger.

- **Boundaries:** Learn to say no. Start with small things—a phone call you don't want to take, a favor you don't want to do. Pay attention to what makes you uncomfortable. State your limits clearly without explaining or apologizing. Protect your space, time, and energy as if they belong to someone you love.

- **Emotional awareness:** Name your feelings as they come up and notice where you feel them in your body. Learn to sit with uncomfortable emotions without trying to fix or avoid them. Understanding your emotional landscape helps you respond to situations rather than react to them.

- **Self-care routines:** Create daily practices that ground you. This isn't about bubble baths; it's about consistent habits that support your mental health. Regular sleep schedules, healthy meals, physical movement, quiet time alone—these basics form the foundation of emotional stability.

Grieving the Lost Past

So much of "grief work" is coming to the realization that we don't ever really "get over" our trauma; instead, we learn to hold ourselves in it with bigger, wider, and softer arms than before.

When we talk about leaving narcissistic relationships, we often focus on the relief of escape and the triumph of breaking free. But there's another side to this story: the deep grief for what was lost. We grieve not just for the relationship that was but for the one we thought we had. We mourn the years we spent believing in false promises, the dreams we built on shifting sand, the person we used to be before the abuse chipped away at our core.

This grief catches us when we least expect it, showing up in quiet moments when we smell a familiar cologne, hear a song that used to mean something to us, or pass by places that hold memories. It comes in waves, strong enough to knock us down just when we think we're standing steady, and that's okay... so okay. Grief, when all's said and done, is proof that you're human, that you had the courage to love deeply, hope sincerely, and trust completely.

Recognizing Grief

Grief is the mind and body's natural response to loss. While most people associate grief with death, it occurs after any significant loss—including the end of relationships and the loss of trust, safety, and identity that comes with narcissistic abuse.

This grief shows up in specific ways. You might have trouble sleeping or sleep too much. Your eating patterns might change. You could feel physically exhausted or experience headaches and muscle tension. Your emotions may swing from anger to sadness to numbness, sometimes all in one day. You might replay memories constantly or have trouble concentrating on daily tasks.

These reactions happen because your brain is processing multiple losses at once: the relationship itself, the future you planned, your sense of self, the time you invested, and the belief that the relationship was real. Your brain needs to reform its understanding of the past and create new expectations for the future.

The Stages of Grief

Grief follows recognizable patterns, though everyone experiences them differently and not always in the same order. Here's what each stage looks like when recovering from narcissistic abuse:

- **Denial:** Denial, as we discussed earlier, is a psychological defense mechanism where your brain actively rejects the reality of abuse. You might downplay serious incidents, rationalize abusive behavior, or convince yourself things aren't as bad as they seem. This happens because accepting the full truth at once would be too overwhelming. Your brain creates distance from the pain to help you function.

- **Anger:** When denial breaks, anger surfaces. This stage involves recognizing the unfairness and intentionality of the abuse. You start seeing how the narcissist deliberately manipulated and hurt you. Your anger can be directed at the abuser, the people who enabled them, the system that failed to protect you, or yourself. This stage marks the beginning of valuing your own rights and boundaries.

- **Bargaining:** In bargaining, you try to negotiate with the past. Your mind searches for ways you could have prevented or changed the outcome. You might obsess over specific moments, thinking that if you'd acted differently, things would have turned out better. This reflects an attempt to regain control over a situation where you had none.

- **Depression:** Depression in grief isn't the same as clinical depression, though they can overlap. This stage involves processing the actual losses: time invested, dreams abandoned, trust broken, identity damaged. You face the full scope of what was taken from you. Your energy drops, hope feels distant, and daily tasks become harder.

- **Acceptance:** Acceptance means acknowledging what happened without trying to change it. You stop fighting against reality or blaming yourself. You see the abuse clearly for what it was—not your fault, not something you could have prevented, not a reflection of your worth. From this understanding, you can begin to rebuild.

These stages aren't a straight line; you might bounce between them, skip some, or revisit others. Each person's experience of grief looks different.

Honoring the Past and Moving Forward

I told a friend a while back that I was going through some old vacation photos. There we were, my daughter and I at the beach, at theme parks, at holiday gatherings. Smiles that didn't quite reach our eyes. Bodies held slightly tense, even in moments that should have been pure joy. She suggested I throw them away. "Why keep reminders of those times?" she asked.

I replied that even though the pain was evident in my tight shoulders, even though my daughter's smile looked careful and measured, there were still moments of truth. The way she squealed when the waves touched her toes for the first time. How she gripped my hand on the carousel, half scared, half thrilled. The sandcastles we built together, both of us learning to create something beautiful even on unstable ground.

The tension in those photos was real. The walking on eggshells was real. The constant calculation of how to avoid conflict was real. But so were the small moments when joy slipped through the cracks and love found its way past fear. Both truths live in those photos, telling the story of how we survived, how we protected our tiny moments of connection despite everything.

The path forward isn't about sorting memories into neat piles of "good" and "bad." It's messier than that. Some days, you'll remember the warmth of those moments, and other days, you'll see the strings that were being pulled behind the scenes. Both perspectives are valid. Both are part of your story.

This is how you move forward; this is how you wake up and fuel yourself with the strength you need to take one foot, put it in front of the other, and keep going:

- You write letters you'll never send, pouring out all the words that got stuck in your throat. Note down the anger, the hurt, the things you wish you'd said. Write until your hand cramps and your tears dry. Then burn the letters, bury them, or lock them away. It doesn't really matter what you do with them; what matters is that you're finally giving voice to your truth.

- You turn your pain into art. Paint your feelings—your anger, your grief, all of the weight that you once carried. Dance out your freedom. Make music from your healing. Art bypasses the logical mind, which wants to explain everything, and lets your emotions speak their own language.

- You can cling to the ritual of remembering what's good, and when it seems as if there's not a lot of good out there for you, you can create it yourself. Plant a garden. Light a candle each night. Take a photo of one beautiful thing each day. Small acts of beauty remind us that life grows even in broken places and that we can make something new from what we've survived.

Acknowledging Your Complex Emotions

Our emotions are a lot easier to understand when we have language for them—when our vocabulary is big enough to hold the full weight of our experience. A simple "I feel sad" or "I feel angry" doesn't do justice to the range of emotions that come with narcissistic abuse.

You might feel rage at the abuser while still missing them. Relief at the fact you're free but shame that you stayed so long. You'll feel pride in your strength alongside grief for the years you lost. You'll love parts of who they were while hating what they did. Your job is to make space for all of these emotions, to let each one tell its part of your story. This honest acknowledgment is what marks the difference between surviving and healing.

Finding Balance

Balance starts with recognition. Notice what triggers intense reactions; it could be criticism at work, conflict with friends, or making decisions. Track these moments, as this will help you prepare for when you're triggered.

Learn to read your emotional temperature. Create a personal scale from 1 to 10, where 1 is completely calm and 10 is overwhelming distress. Check in with yourself throughout the day. When you hit a 7, you know it's time to use your coping tools to avoid reaching 10.

Build a set of reliable responses. Different intensity levels need different tools: Mild anxiety might need a walk, moderate distress might require talking to a friend, while severe episodes might call for professional support. Having this tool kit ready prevents emotional spirals. For instance:

- **For mild distress (levels 1–3):** Use simple physical tools. Step outside for fresh air. Turn on music that changes your mood. Move your body—stretch, walk, dance. These small actions can shift your emotional state before it intensifies.

- **For moderate distress (levels 4–6):** Engage your mind actively. Write down what triggered you and what you're feeling. Talk to someone who understands narcissistic abuse. Use grounding techniques such as counting backward from 100. These tools help break the cycle of escalating emotions.

- **For high distress (levels 7–8):** Set firm boundaries. Remove yourself from triggering situations. Call your therapist or support group. Take a mental health day if needed. Your recovery comes first.

- **For crisis levels (9–10):** Have an emergency plan ready. Keep phone numbers for crisis hotlines, your therapist, and trusted friends where you can find them easily. Know which emergency rooms near you have mental health services. Remember that reaching out isn't weakness—it's wisdom.

Trauma-Related Symptoms

The brain might remember, but the body does too. Trauma from narcissistic abuse isn't just stored in your memories—it lives in your muscles, your nerves, your gut. Your body keeps score of every time you tensed up while waiting for your abuser to come home, every moment you held your breath waiting for their reaction, and every night you couldn't sleep because of the knot in your stomach.

This physical memory shows up in real symptoms. Your heart races when you hear a certain tone of voice. Your shoulders tighten when someone stands too close. Your digestion acts up when you face conflict. Your sleep becomes unpredictable. These aren't signs of weakness or proof that you're "too sensitive"; they're your body's natural response to prolonged stress and fear.

Combat veterans and survivors of abuse often share similar physical reactions because trauma affects the nervous system in specific ways. When you spend months or years in survival mode, your body's alarm system stays switched on. Even after you're safe, your body remembers to stay alert, stay ready, stay guarded.

Here are five key trauma symptoms from narcissistic abuse:

- **Hypervigilance:** Your nervous system stays on high alert, making you scan rooms for exits, startle at sudden movements, and notice tiny changes in people's expressions or tone. This is because your brain has learned to spot signs of danger to protect you from the narcissist's unpredictable behavior.

- **Dissociation:** You feel disconnected from your body or surroundings, like you're watching life through a fog, and time might seem to skip or slow down. This mental "checking out" began as a survival tool when the abuse felt too intense to handle consciously.

- **Sleep disruption:** Your sleep patterns change dramatically as you struggle with falling asleep, wake up throughout the night, or experience vivid nightmares because your body has learned to stay alert for danger, even during rest.

- **Somatic pain:** Physical pain shows up in your body without any clear medical cause, often appearing as headaches, muscle tension, a clenched jaw, or stomach problems. Prolonged stress and fear create real physical responses in your nervous system.

- **Emotional flooding:** You experience sudden, overwhelming waves of emotion that feel out of proportion to current events. A small trigger—a song, a phrase, a gesture—can unleash intense feelings from past trauma, making it hard to stay present in the moment.

Self-Care Tools

If you want to change, you're going to have to be willing to let go of survival mode. This means learning new tools to take care of yourself—real tools, not just temporary escapes:

- **Body scan:** Take 10 minutes each day to check in with your body from head to toe, noticing areas of tension or discomfort without trying to fix them. Give yourself permission to release what you find, because your body needs to learn that it's safe now.

- **Sensory grounding:** When anxiety or flashbacks hit, deliberately engage your senses by touching something cold, smelling some essential oils, or listening to specific music that anchors you to the present moment and pulls you back from the past.

- **Movement release:** Find ways to discharge stored trauma through movement by shaking out your limbs, dancing without rules, or taking walks in nature. Trauma gets stuck in the body and needs physical ways to flow out.

- **Boundary setting:** Practice saying no to small things first, then work your way up to bigger boundaries by listening to your gut reactions and honoring what makes you uncomfortable, even if you can't explain why.

- **Time blocking:** Create a schedule that puts you first by setting specific times for rest, meals, and activities that recharge you. You need to relearn that your time belongs to you now, not to someone else's demands.

Overcoming Denial and Self-Blame

The shame that you're carrying isn't yours to own. It belongs to the person who manipulated you, controlled you, and made you doubt yourself. Yet so many survivors of narcissistic abuse walk around weighted down by blame that was never theirs to carry.

Think about it—no one chooses to be abused. No one walks into a relationship wanting to lose themselves. You didn't cause someone else to choose to manipulate and control you. Their actions reflect their character, not your worth.

The voice in your head that tells you, "Maybe it was my fault" or "I should have known better" isn't your voice. It's gaslighting, the result of years spent being told that everything was your fault. That voice grew stronger every time you were made to apologize for someone else's behavior, every time you were told you were "too sensitive," every time you were blamed for someone else's choices.

Breaking free from self-blame means challenging these thoughts each time they surface. It means asking yourself: "Would I blame a friend in this situation? Would I tell them they deserved abuse? Would I say they should have tried harder to fix someone else's behavior?"

Here's how to break free from this shame and self-blame:

- Catch shame statements when they pop up. Notice when you say things like, "I let this happen" or "I was stupid to stay." These thoughts feel true because you've thought them so many times, but they're not facts—they're learned responses from abuse.

- Replace these thoughts with reality checks. When you hear yourself say, "I should have left sooner," ask yourself, "With what money? With what support? When I was being monitored? When I was afraid for my safety?" See how the full picture changes the story.

- Write down specific examples of times you tried to make things better. List the conversations you had, the therapy you suggested, the changes you made. This evidence shows you didn't "let" anything happen; instead, you were actively trying to fix a situation that someone else was actively breaking.

- Look at photos of yourself from that time. Notice your eyes, your smile, your posture. Observe yourself with the same compassion you'd feel for a friend. That person in the photos was doing their best with the information and resources they had at the time.

- Keep a record of the facts. Not your ex's version, not your self-blame version, but the actual events. What was said? What was done? Looking at actions instead of interpretations helps cut through the fog of self-blame.

Chapter 3

Laying the Foundations
for Healing

"You look great," my friend said six months after I'd left. I nodded and smiled, but inside, I thought, If you only knew.

No one really understood how bad it had been at the start. I had become so skilled at hiding the pain that most people didn't see it. They didn't know about the nights I cried alone in the bathroom, careful that no one could hear. They didn't notice how I jumped at sudden noises or how I'd lie awake at 3 a.m., staring at the ceiling and replaying conversations with my ex.

Yes, I was sleeping better. Yes, I was trying to go out again. I was reconnecting with friends, hosting gatherings, and redecorating my home in a way that felt like me again.

But despite these steps forward, some days the heaviness still settled in my chest—the kind that made me want to hide away in my closet and cry, a weight in my heart that no one could see.

Recovery isn't a straight line. It's made up of quiet victories no one else notices—small choices that feel like giant leaps. Moments when you catch yourself laughing and realize you no longer feel guilty for it.

These are the true building blocks of healing—not the grand breakthroughs people expect, but the tiny moments when you choose yourself, trust yourself, and start becoming yourself again.

One decision. One day. One breath at a time.

Mindfulness and Meditation

Meditation saved my life. It was the only thing that kept me sane and allowed me to survive the emotional turmoil of being in a relationship with a narcissist.

I first came to meditation by accident—literally. One day, I was feeling so anxious, so overwhelmed by my emotions, that I didn't know how to handle it. I'd just dropped my daughter off at preschool, and I couldn't bring myself to go home and be alone with my thoughts. My emotions felt so dysregulated that I needed the presence of a four-year-old just to feel grounded.

Instead of going home, I went to a bookstore. I'd been searching for a specific book on meditation, something I'd heard about from a group that offered meditation practices. But as I walked through the aisles, I picked up the wrong book—one with a title so similar to the one I was looking for that I didn't realize my mistake until later.

At first, I was disappointed. But as I flipped through the pages, I found something unexpected: a simple phrase in the book's foreword. That phrase became my lifeline. I started repeating it over and over, using it as an anchor to keep my mind from spiraling. In those early days, I wasn't practicing meditation in any formal way. I was just holding on to something that brought me comfort and kept me present.

If you're just beginning your healing journey, you don't need anything complicated. You don't need to master advanced techniques or sit in silence for hours. Meditation can be as simple as repeating a phrase that brings you peace or focusing on your breath for a few moments at a time.

Later, I dove deeper into mindfulness and meditation, exploring practices that transformed my life in profound ways. But in the beginning, all I needed was something small and manageable—that was enough to start the journey.

As you begin to heal from your relationship, start where you are. Keep it simple. You don't need to do anything complicated to see results—just something that brings you back to yourself, one breath at a time..

Meditation Techniques

There are different types of meditation, and each has its own flavor and its own way of helping you find stillness. It's important to remain consistent with the practice you choose. Experiment with the options provided in this book and determine which one resonates with you the most. Once you've decided on one, practice it for a few weeks. Aim to incorporate it into your daily routine; this can be as simple as taking a few deep breaths upon waking or repeating an affirmation before bedtime. Remember, everyone is unique, so feel free to explore these practices.

Guided meditation is a structured practice where an instructor leads participants through a specific mental journey or body awareness exercise. The guide uses their voice to direct attention to different aspects of experience: physical sensations, breath patterns, emotional states, or visualizations. This method is particularly effective for beginners as it provides a clear structure and continuous support throughout the practice.

Mantra meditation is a focused concentration practice that uses the repetition of a specific sound, word, or phrase. The mantra serves as an object of attention, training the mind to maintain a steady focus while letting go of distracting thoughts. Practitioners choose a mantra that resonates with them personally or work with traditional Sanskrit phrases. The repetitive nature of this practice helps to quiet mental chatter and supports the development of deeper concentration.

Loving-kindness meditation is a systematic practice for developing compassion, known traditionally as "metta" meditation. Practitioners cultivate positive emotions through specific phrases directed first toward themselves, then progressively toward others.

The practice follows a structured sequence: self, loved ones, neutral individuals, difficult people, and finally all beings. This method specifically targets emotional well-being and interpersonal relationships.

I have found all these types of meditations to be helpful and amazing in their own right, but loving-kindness meditation has a special place in my heart because it taught me how to be gentle with myself again. After years of harsh self-judgment, its simple phrases became a pathway back to self-compassion.

Here's a loving kindness meditation you can try. Find a quiet space and sit comfortably. Take a few deep breaths to settle in. Place one hand on your heart if this feels right. Then direct these phrases toward yourself:

- I honor my strength in surviving.
- I trust my heart to heal.
- I give myself permission to rest.
- I welcome joy back into my life.

The power lies not just in the words but in giving yourself permission to believe them. Let each phrase sink in. Some days, they'll feel impossible. Other days, they'll bring tears. Sometimes, they'll feel like coming home to yourself.

When your mind drifts to old doubts or criticism, notice this without judgment. Return to the phrases. Return to this moment. Return to yourself.

Breathing Exercises

There were days when I felt that it was much safer to not breathe. That if I held my breath for long enough, I could shrink myself into invisibility, making myself small enough to avoid notice and quiet enough to avoid criticism. I learned to take shallow breaths and to live in that space between breaths where nothing could touch me.

But breath is life. Each inhale is your body's way of claiming space in the world. Every exhale is a release of what no longer serves you. Learning to breathe fully again entails permitting and teaching yourself to take up space, make noise, and let yourself be seen.

Our breath patterns tell the story of our nervous system. Short, shallow breaths speak of anxiety and fear. Held breath tells of frozen trauma. Deep, full breaths signal to our body that we're safe, that we can relax, that we can finally let go.

Here are some breathing exercises that can help you reclaim your relationship with breath.

Diaphragmatic breathing is a deep breathing exercise that fully engages the diaphragm and increases the capacity of your lungs to take in oxygen. This type of breathing turns on your body's natural relaxation response, slowing your heart rate and lowering your blood pressure.

How to practice diaphragmatic breathing:

1.   Lie on your back on a flat surface.

2. Place one hand on your chest and the other just below your rib cage.

3. Breathe in slowly through your nose, feeling your belly expand while your chest remains still.

4. Tighten your stomach muscles and let them fall inward as you exhale through pursed lips.

5. The hand on your chest should stay relatively still, while the hand on your belly will rise and fall.

Start with five to ten minutes of practice. As you get comfortable, you can practice diaphragmatic breathing while sitting up, then eventually while standing or even walking.

Box breathing creates a rhythm of equal counts that helps to regulate your nervous system. Used by military personnel and anxiety specialists, this technique brings your breathing into a balanced pattern that calms both mind and body.

How to practice box breathing:

1. Find a comfortable seated position with your back supported.

2. Relax your shoulders down and away from your ears.

3. Keep your feet flat on the floor.

4. Begin by exhaling all the air from your lungs.

5. Inhale through your nose for a count of four, feeling your belly expand.

6. Hold your breath for a count of four without tensing.

7. Exhale through your mouth for a count of four, emptying your lungs completely.

8. Hold the empty breath for a count of four.

9. Repeat this cycle for four to five rounds.

Start with just two to three minutes. You can gradually increase the duration as it becomes more comfortable.

4–7–8 breathing works as a natural tranquilizer for your nervous system by extending your exhale. This pattern helps to release deep-seated tension and can be particularly useful for sleep or anxiety.

How to practice 4–7–8 breathing:

1. Sit with your back straight or lie down flat.

2. Place the tip of your tongue against the ridge behind your upper front teeth.

3. Exhale completely through your mouth, making a "whoosh" sound.

4. Close your mouth and inhale quietly through your nose for four counts.

5. Hold your breath for seven counts.

6. Exhale completely through your mouth for eight counts, making the "whoosh" sound again.

7. This completes one breath cycle.

Begin with four cycles and gradually work up to eight. Practice this twice a day, and never do more than eight cycles at a time in your first month of practice.

Building a Support Network

People. We're richest when we have people around us—those friends who will, without ever batting an eyelid, bring us soup when we're sick, pick up our kids in emergencies, or sit with us through endless cups of coffee while we tell the same story for the tenth time. After narcissistic abuse, these connections become more than comfort; they become oxygen.

But here's the hard truth: Some of your old friends might not be there anymore. The narcissist made sure of that. They whispered doubts about your friends, created conflicts, and made socializing so difficult that you gave up. Maybe you even pushed people away yourself, tired of making excuses for why you couldn't meet, why you had to cancel again, why you seemed so different.

Now, it's time to rebuild. Not just your inner circle, but your trust in people. It's time to remember that not every outstretched hand holds a hidden agenda, that not every kind word comes with strings attached, and that safe people exist.

Your Safe People

Safe people prove their trustworthiness through consistent actions. They show up for the quiet pain, the small victories, and the everyday rebuilding of your life.

What makes someone safe?

- They honor your boundaries with grace. A simple "no" from you receives acceptance and respect.

- They welcome your full range of emotions. Your anger has space. Your grief has time. Your joy is celebrated.

- They hold your story sacred. Your experiences stay private, protected in the trust you've given them.

- They bring steady, reliable energy. Each interaction feels clear and consistent. Their kindness flows from genuine care.

- They take responsibility for their actions. Direct, honest apologies follow their mistakes.

- They cheer your growing strength. Your independence makes them happy. Your success brings them joy.

Check Your Potential Support People

Take a moment to think about the people in your life right now. Some might have stuck with you through the worst moments. Others might be new connections you're just starting to trust. Use these questions to reflect on who belongs in your circle of trust:

- How well do they listen when you share?
- Can they stay present in difficult moments?
- How do they respond to your choices?
- Are they dependable in daily life?
- How do you feel after spending time with them?
- How do they handle their own mistakes?

Developing Authentic Connections

Good relationships aren't stumbled upon, or found, or gifted to us by fate. They're built, one honest conversation at a time, one kept promise after another, one moment of genuine connection building on the last.

It takes a lot of courage to open your heart up again, to decide that the pain of your past isn't going to get in the way and prevent you from meeting exceptional people. Yes, you've learned to guard yourself, watch for red flags, and question every kindness. But real connection starts with small risks: showing a piece of your true self, speaking an honest thought, sharing a genuine feeling.

Here's how to build authentic relationships:

- **Start with self-trust:** Learn to trust your own reactions again. Notice when you feel comfortable or uncomfortable with someone. Honor those feelings. Your intuition grew sharper through your experience—it's trying to protect you.

- **Open up gradually:** Share small truths first. Maybe tell someone about your day, a simple preference, or a minor frustration. Watch how they receive these pieces of you. Do they listen? Remember? Respect what you share?

- **Practice being present:** Focus on the current moment with people. Notice when past hurts make you withdraw or future fears make you defensive. Remind yourself that this interaction is new, with a different person.

- **Set clear expectations:** Say what you need. If you want someone to just listen, tell them. If you need space, name it. Clear communication builds trust and shows others how to be trustworthy with you.

Maintaining Boundaries in Relationships

The people whom we love and who love us won't push us away or crucify us for having boundaries. Instead, they'll respect those boundaries, honor them, and help us protect them. After years of having your boundaries trampled by a narcissist, this might sound impossible to believe. But healthy relationships thrive on clear limits and mutual respect.

Think about a garden. The fence around it doesn't just keep things out; it creates a safe space for growth. Your boundaries work the same way. They mark where you end and others begin. They protect your energy, your time, and your peace of mind. They tell people how to treat you.

You might feel guilty at first. Setting boundaries after narcissistic abuse often triggers old fears: What if they get angry? What if they leave? What if I'm asking for too much? Remember that someone's reaction to your boundaries tells you everything about them and nothing about whether your boundaries are valid. Here's how you can effectively enforce your boundaries:

- **Start with your non-negotiables:** Identify what you absolutely need to feel safe and respected. Maybe it's having phone calls returned within a day. Maybe it's not being yelled at. Maybe it's having your "no" accepted without pressure. These become your baseline boundaries.

- **Name your feelings:** Learn to say, "I feel uncomfortable when..." or "It bothers me if..." Don't justify or overexplain. Your feelings matter simply because you feel them.

- **Set clear limits:** Be direct about what works for you: "I need advance notice before plans." "I prefer to be asked before you share my personal information." "I'm not available after 9 p.m. unless it's an emergency."

- **Enforce your boundaries consistently:** When someone crosses a line, address it immediately. A simple "That doesn't work for me" or "Please don't do that" is enough. If they continue, step back from the relationship. Your boundaries only work if you maintain them.

- **Accept the reactions:** Some people won't like your new limits. They might push back, act hurt, or try to make you feel guilty. Their discomfort isn't your responsibility. Someone who truly cares about you will respect your boundaries, even if they don't understand them.

Engaging in Self-Compassion Practices

Self-compassion is a practice that says every scar tells a story of survival, not shame. After narcissistic abuse, this feels like learning a foreign language. Your internal narrator has borrowed the narcissist's voice for so long that kindness toward yourself sounds false and feels wrong.

My ex always made comments about what I ate, despite my efforts to maintain a healthy diet as a personal trainer. He would often say, "You look great," but would then make remarks about my food choices, implying that I was wrong for eating certain things or that I was indulging too much, often in a passive-aggressive manner. After he moved out, I began buying ice cream for my movie nights alone at home. During the holidays, when he came back to visit with our daughter, I went to get some ice cream as usual. He laughed heartily and said, "Ice cream?" as if I was committing a crime. I chose not to respond or explain, but I felt a tightness inside that I hadn't noticed when we were together. It dawned on me that ice cream represented more than just a sweet treat; it was a symbol of my newfound freedom. It reminded me of the movie *Sleeping with the Enemy*, when Julia Roberts's character straightens the towels as a subconscious habit and then, upon realizing her abusive husband is no longer there, messes them up and smiles.

So, what I know is that rebuilding a relationship with yourself takes more than positive thinking. It takes concrete tools and daily practices that slowly replace the critic in your head with a voice of reason and compassion. Here's where we start.

Positive Self-Talk

Replace statements like "I should have known better" with "I know better now." Train your mind to spot when you're using the narcissist's words against yourself. When you catch thoughts like *I'm too sensitive* or *I can't do anything right*, stop. Ask yourself: "Whose voice is this really? Would I talk to someone I love this way?"

Write down every critical thought for a week. Next to each one, write what you'd tell your best friend in the same situation. *I was stupid for staying* becomes "You were doing your best with the information you had." *I fell for their lies* becomes "They deliberately manipulated you; that's on them, not you."

Notice your daily victories, no matter how small. Made a decision without asking anyone else? Victory. Spoke up in a meeting? Victory. Trusted your gut about someone? Victory. Each of these moments proves you're rebuilding trust in yourself.

Use phrases that build you up: "I trust my judgment." "My feelings are valid." "I know what's best for me." These aren't empty affirmations; they're declarations of truth that counter years of programming. Say them until you believe them. Then say them until they become your natural response.

Self-Reflection

Set aside time each day to check in with yourself—not just your surface thoughts but deeper truths. Ask yourself: "What made me tense up today? When did I feel most like myself? Which old patterns tried to creep back in?" This isn't about judging your responses but understanding them.

Keep two kinds of records. First, track your triggers: situations, words, or behaviors that send you back into survival mode. Maybe it's someone raising their voice, feeling rushed to make a decision, or hearing "You're too sensitive." Second, track your responses: Did you freeze? Fight back? Shut down? This mapping helps you spot patterns and prepare for them in future.

Pay attention to your body's signals. Where do you hold stress? When does your breathing change? What makes your shoulders tense or your stomach tight? Your body often recognizes threats before your mind catches up. Learning to read these signals helps you respond rather than react.

Watch for signs of growth that others might miss. Did you speak up instead of staying quiet? Trust your memory instead of doubting it? Choose your own preference instead of deferring to someone else? These small shifts mark big internal changes. Write them down. On hard days, read them back to yourself as proof of how far you've come.

Self-Forgiveness

Self-forgiveness is allowing yourself to release the weight of blame you've been carrying. Maybe you think you should have seen the signs earlier, left sooner, been stronger, known better. But you did what you could with what you knew at the time.

Look back at your younger self—the one who believed in love, who tried to make things work, and who hoped things would change. That person deserves your compassion, not your criticism. They were fighting battles you can only now understand. They were doing their best with limited tools and information.

Start by forgiving yourself for small things. Forgive yourself for the times you doubted your own memory, for the moments you made yourself smaller to keep the peace, and for believing the lies you were told. Each act of self-forgiveness loosens the grip of shame.

Remember: Staying wasn't weakness; it was survival. The same strength that kept you alive then is helping you heal now. You don't need to carry the burden of someone else's choices. Their actions reflect their character, not your worth

Setting Realistic Recovery Goals

I think most of us expect ourselves to "get over it" so quickly, to bounce back, to just move on. After all, that's what everyone seems to tell us: "It's in the past now" or "You're free; be happy!" But recovery from narcissistic abuse isn't about snapping back like a rubber band. It's about rebuilding yourself piece by piece.

Your recovery goals need to match where you really are, not where others think you should be. Some days, getting out of bed and taking a shower is a win. Other days, you might feel strong enough to tackle bigger challenges: setting boundaries with family, starting therapy, or speaking your truth out loud.

The trick is to set goals that stretch you but don't break you. Goals that acknowledge both where you are and where you want to be. Goals that measure success by your standards, not someone else's timeline.

Let me show you how to create recovery goals that actually serve your healing.

Start With Your Current Reality

Take an honest look at where you are right now. Rate different areas of your life: sleep, anxiety levels, ability to work, social connections, self-trust. Don't judge the numbers—they're just information to help you plan.

Break Down Big Goals

Instead of "Heal from trauma," aim for smaller steps:

- **Week 1:** Write down three things that weren't your fault.
- **Month 1:** Attend one support group meeting.
- **Month 3:** Share your story with one trusted person.
- **Month 6:** Learn to sit with uncomfortable emotions for five minutes.

Make Goals Specific and Measurable

Change "Become more confident" to "Make one decision daily without asking others' opinions." Turn "Trust myself" into "Check in with my gut feeling once a day and write down what it tells me."

Set Time Frames That Make Sense

During your early recovery, you'll need shorter-term goals—think day by day or week by week. As you get stronger, you can look further ahead. But keep checking: Are these time frames adding pressure or providing structure?

Include Self-Care Goals

Plan for setbacks by building in recovery time:

- Schedule regular rest days.
- Set limits on the emotional energy you spend.
- Create space between challenging tasks.
- Allow yourself to step back when needed.

Track Progress Your Way

Maybe it's journaling, maybe it's talking to a friend, or maybe it's using a simple scale from one to ten. Find what works for you to notice small changes over time.

There's a Japanese saying that goes, "Fall seven times, stand up eight." After narcissistic abuse, this might feel impossible. Some days, just getting up once feels like moving mountains. But here's what I've learned: Healing isn't about never falling. It's about learning to trust that you can get back up.

The foundation you build now, your support system, your boundaries, your self-compassion, your safety plan—these aren't just tools for survival but the building blocks of your new life. Each small step you take, each boundary you set, each moment you choose yourself adds another stone to this foundation.

Remember: You're not just healing from what happened. You're building something new. Something stronger. Something that's truly yours. And while the path isn't always clear, you're not walking it alone anymore.

Chapter 4

Building Resilience
and Self-Esteem

There's a difference between surviving and thriving. Survival got you through the abuse—you learned to duck, to dodge, to make yourself small enough to avoid attention. But thriving? That's about standing tall again, taking up space, and letting yourself be seen. It's about transforming from someone who endures to someone who flourishes.

During the abuse, you developed perfect instincts for survival. You knew exactly which topics to avoid, which moods meant danger, and which words would start a fight. You became an expert at reading rooms, managing emotions that weren't yours, and shrinking your needs to avoid conflict. These skills kept you alive, but they also kept you trapped.

Now it's time to learn new skills. Not the hypervigilant ones that protected you then, but the bold ones that will free you now. Skills like trusting your judgment, expressing your needs, and believing in your worth. Skills that turn survival mode into growth mode.

Identifying Personal Strengths

You were you before them; you were you before the narcissist tried to remake you in their image. You had dreams, talents, quirks, and passions. You had a laugh that came straight from your belly, opinions you didn't second-guess, and a spark in your eyes that was all your own.

The narcissist didn't erase these parts of you—they just buried them under layers of doubt and fear. Think of your strengths like muscles that haven't been used in a while. They might feel weak now, and they might shake when you first try to use them, but they're still there. The courage that helped you face each day, the creativity that found ways to cope, the resilience that kept your spirit alive—these strengths didn't disappear. They grew stronger.

Now it's time to rediscover who you are without the narcissist's voice in your head, and to remember what makes you uniquely you.

Finding Your Strengths

Start with what got you through. Think about the hardest days of abuse—which qualities kept you going? Maybe it was determination, resourcefulness, or the ability to find hope in small moments. These aren't just survival tactics. They're proof of your inner strength.

Look at your current life. What do people count on you for? Maybe you're the friend who always knows what to say, the parent who creates magic from simple moments, or the colleague who stays calm in chaos. These everyday abilities point to deeper strengths.

Ask trusted friends or family: "When do you see me at my best?" Their answers might surprise you. Often, others spot our strengths before we do. One friend told me she admired how I could find humor even in dark times. I'd never seen that as a strength; I thought I was just coping. But she was right— finding light in darkness is a gift.

Write it all down:

- skills that helped you survive
- natural abilities you've always had
- qualities others value in you
- challenges you've overcome
- moments you're proud of

Keep this list where you can see it. Add to it as you remember or discover more strengths. These aren't just words on paper—they're reminders of who you really are.

Reflection Exercises

Sit quietly with these questions:

- When did you feel most alive before the abuse?
- What problems do people often ask you to help solve?
- What feels natural and effortless to you?

- When do you lose track of time because you're so absorbed? Write down your first thoughts without editing.

Take a "day in the life" inventory. At the end of each day for a week, write down the following:

- three things you handled well
- one moment when you felt confident
- one challenge you faced
- how you dealt with it

Feedback From Others

Start with people you trust. Ask them: "What strengths do you see in me?" "When have you seen me at my best?" "What do you admire about how I've handled this past year?"

You can also create a "story circle" with close friends or family:

1. Share a challenging moment from your past.
2. Ask them to point out the strengths they hear in your story.
3. Listen for patterns in their feedback.
4. Write down what surprises you about their perspective.

Notice how you react to positive feedback. If you find yourself dismissing compliments or doubting praise, that's normal after narcissistic abuse. Write down the feedback anyway, and come back to it later when your defenses are lower.

Challenging Self-Critical Thoughts

Instead of saying, "I'm not good enough," I've started saying, "My inner critic is loud today." Instead of saying, "I'm so selfish," I've started saying, "My inner critic is speaking from old wounds." These aren't just word games; they're ways to separate your true voice from the one the narcissist planted in your head.

Think about it—when did you start believing you weren't enough? When did taking care of yourself become "selfish"? These thoughts have a history. They have an address. They came from somewhere, from someone. They're not facts about who you are—they're echoes of what you were told to believe.

Your inner critic borrowed its script from your abuser. It learned their lines by heart. But here's the thing about scripts: They can be rewritten. You can learn to catch these thoughts mid-sentence. To question them. To talk back to them.

Let me show you how to challenge these thoughts one by one.

Cognitive Restructuring

Cognitive restructuring is a therapeutic technique that helps you identify, challenge, and change distorted thought patterns. These distorted thoughts—like "I'm worthless" or "Everything is my fault"—affect how you feel and act. The goal is to replace these distorted thoughts with more balanced, realistic ones based on actual evidence.

After narcissistic abuse, your mind often processes information through filters created by trauma. You might automatically assume criticism in neutral comments, expect rejection in every relationship, or blame yourself for others' actions. Cognitive restructuring helps you recognize these filters and adjust them.

The process has specific steps:

1. Notice your automatic thoughts when you feel upset.
2. Identify the distortion in these thoughts.
3. Challenge the evidence supporting these thoughts.
4. Create alternative, more balanced thoughts based on the complete evidence.

Essentially, it's like debugging faulty code in your mental programming, finding where the errors crept in and correcting them one by one.

Below is a concrete example of cognitive restructuring in action.

Situation: A friend doesn't respond to your text for two days.

Your automatic thought is, *They hate me. I must have done something wrong. I'm too needy, just like my ex always said.*

To break this down:

1. **Identify the distortion:**
   o Jumping to Conclusions (assuming You Know Why They Haven't Responded)
   o Personalizing (making It About You)
   o Using your abuser's voice ("too needy")

2. **Examine the evidence for the thought:**
   o   They haven't responded.
   o   I feel anxious about this.
3. **Examine the evidence against the thought:**
   o   They've been reliable in the past.
   o   Last week, they invited me to dinner.
   o   They mentioned being busy at work.
   o   They've taken time to respond before.
4. **Create a balanced thought:** *My friend hasn't responded yet. This makes me anxious because of my past experiences. But they might be busy, and their silence likely has nothing to do with me. I can check in again if I don't hear back tomorrow.*

See how this shifts from an emotional reaction based on past trauma to a more realistic assessment based on current evidence?

Mindfulness Practices

I turned to mindfulness and meditation while still in my marriage. These practices became my lifeline, a secret room I could retreat to when everything felt overwhelming. They didn't fix my relationship, but they helped me survive it for another 13 years.

The irony wasn't lost on me; I became so passionate about meditation that I eventually trained as a teacher. The wellness studio I opened (the one he claimed people only visited "out of pity") became a place where I taught fitness, yoga, and meditation. I've even written books on mindfulness under different names.

I share this because I know many of you have probably tried similar paths. We read self-help books, download meditation apps, take yoga classes, all in the hope that if we can just become "better" somehow, our relationship will improve too. If we're just calmer, more patient, more understanding, maybe they'll stop hurting us. Maybe we'll finally be enough.

Mindfulness and meditation are powerful tools, but not because they'll help you tolerate the intolerable. Their real power comes from helping you see clearly what's happening, teaching you to trust your perceptions again, and giving you the strength to make difficult choices from a place of clarity rather than reactivity.

Body Scanning

This is a systematic practice of paying attention to different parts of your body, one area at a time. This technique helps you notice physical sensations you usually ignore and understand how emotions show up in your body. Many people store stress and trauma physically—tight shoulders, clenched jaw, upset stomach—without realizing it.

How to do it: Lie or sit comfortably. Close your eyes. Start with your toes. Notice any sensations—warmth, coolness, tingling, pressure. Move to your feet, then your ankles, and slowly work up your body. Don't try to relax or change anything; just notice what's there. When you find tension, observe it without judgment. Take about fifteen to twenty minutes to scan your whole body.

Mindful Breathing

This approach is a focused attention practice using breath as an anchor. Unlike deep breathing exercises that try to change your breathing, mindful breathing is about observing your natural breath pattern. This helps calm your nervous system and builds your ability to stay present.

How to do it: Find a quiet spot. Sit or lie comfortably. Notice where you feel your breath most clearly; observe your nostrils, chest, or belly. Don't try to control it—just watch it as if you're watching waves on a beach. When your mind wanders (it will), gently return your attention to your breath. Start with five minutes and gradually increase the time.

Grounding Through Senses

With this exercise, you use your five senses to pull you out of overwhelming thoughts or emotions and into the present moment. This practice helps when you feel disconnected from reality or caught in anxiety spirals.

How to do it: Start with sight, and name specific things you see around you, including colors and details. Move through each sense deliberately. Touch different textures. Listen for distinct sounds. Notice smells in your environment. Finally, focus on taste—even if it's just noticing the taste in your mouth. Be specific with each observation.

Mindful Movement

This approach focuses your attention on physical movement. Unlike regular exercise, the goal isn't fitness; it's connecting with your body's experience of motion. This helps rebuild your bodily awareness and trust in physical sensations.

How to do it: Choose a simple movement, such as walking, stretching, or even washing dishes. Focus completely on the physical experience. With walking, notice how your weight shifts, how your feet feel, and how your arms swing. Don't try to move differently—just notice how you naturally move.

Journaling Prompts

If words are medicine for the soul, then journaling—well, writing in general—has got to be one of the most potent prescriptions we have. Writing helps us make sense of chaos, find patterns in confusion, and speak truths we've kept buried.

When we journal, we're able to have honest conversations with ourselves, perhaps for the first time in years. Each blank page offers us space to explore our thoughts without judgment, to feel emotions without apology, to tell our story in our own voice.

It isn't always easy to find what you want to write about or to know where to start when facing a blank page. Sometimes, we need a gentle push, a question that opens the door to deeper reflection. Here are prompts to guide your writing:

- What made me feel strong today?

- When do I feel most like myself?

- What would I say to my younger self?

- What boundaries do I need to set?

- If I could tell someone exactly how I feel, without consequences, what would I say?

- What am I proud of myself for?

- What do I want my life to look like one year from now?

- When did I last feel truly peaceful?

- What does safety feel like to me?

- Which parts of myself did I hide during the relationship?

- What small victory am I celebrating today?

- What do I need right now that I'm afraid to ask for?

- When did I last trust my gut feeling? What happened?

- Which old beliefs about myself am I ready to let go of?

- What would I do differently if I knew no one would judge me?

There's no right or wrong way to respond to these prompts; just allow yourself to write long paragraphs or short sentences, or to use bullet points or stream of consciousness. Draw pictures if words feel too hard. The goal is expression, not perfection.

Practicing Self-Affirmation Techniques

When I'm in a low place or having a hard day, I go to a mirror, look at myself, and remind myself of what I've survived. I look into my own eyes—sometimes for a few seconds, sometimes longer—and I speak to myself with the same kindness I'd offer a friend who's hurting.

I say simple truths like, "You're here. You made it. You're stronger than you know." None of these are empty phrases; they're statements grounded in fact. I did survive. I am here. My strength isn't something I need to create; it's something I've already proven.

Self-affirmation isn't about convincing yourself that everything's perfect. It's about acknowledging your reality while holding space for your resilience. It's about speaking to yourself in a voice that heals instead of hurts.

Here are some specific affirmation techniques that can help you rebuild your relationship with yourself.

Mirror Work

Standing in front of your reflection is helpful for self-connection. Most people avoid their own gaze or see themselves through harsh, critical eyes. Mirror work challenges this pattern. Start by meeting your own eyes for just a few seconds, then gradually build to longer periods. Speak directly to yourself using present-tense statements that feel true: "I trust my judgment" or "I speak my truth."

Voice Recording

Your inner critic often speaks in your own voice, replays old, doubt-filled messages, and creates new audio messages. Creating voice recordings helps override this negative soundtrack. Find a quiet spot where you won't be interrupted and record simple, true statements about your strength and wisdom. Listen to these recordings during tough moments or as part of your morning routine. The sound of your own voice speaking support is a powerful counter to self-doubt.

Evidence Building

Make your affirmations more solid by collecting real proof of their truth. Keep a dedicated notebook for documenting moments that challenge your negative beliefs. When you say, "I am capable," write down three specific times you handled something difficult. Include dates, conversations, and outcomes. This creates a record you can return to when doubt creeps in.

Setting Boundaries With Self-Love

Boundary work is holy work, important work; it's soul work because it demands that we finally choose ourselves. Not in the selfish way we've been accused of, and not in a way that dismisses others' needs, but in a way that honors our right to exist as whole beings with our own limits and needs.

For too long, your boundaries were labeled as walls. Your "no" was called stubborn. Your limits were seen as threats. You learned to fold yourself smaller, stretch yourself thinner, and twist yourself into shapes that pleased others while your own edges blurred and faded.

But boundaries aren't walls; they're maps. They mark the sacred territory of your soul, showing others how to treat you and showing you how to honor yourself. They say: "This is where I begin. This is what I need. This is what I will and won't accept."

Let's explore how to draw these maps with love instead of fear.

Understanding Boundaries

Boundaries define the physical, emotional, and mental limits we set to protect our well-being and define our relationships with others. They mark which behaviors we'll accept, how we'll allow others to treat us, and how we'll respond when our limits are crossed.

There are various types of boundaries:

- **Physical boundaries** protect your body, personal space, and privacy. They include your right to refuse physical touch, decide who can be close to you, and control your physical environment. Physical boundaries also cover your belongings, your home, and your right to rest.

- **Emotional boundaries** guard your feelings and energy. They involve choosing who gets to know your inner thoughts, when to share feelings, and how much emotional support you can give. Emotional boundaries help you separate your feelings from those of other people and prevent emotional manipulation.

- **Mental boundaries** protect your thoughts, values, and opinions. They involve your right to your own beliefs, the ability to disagree with others, and the freedom to change your mind. Mental boundaries keep others from forcing their thoughts or beliefs on you.

- **Time boundaries** protect how you spend your time and energy. They involve saying no to extra commitments, deciding when to be available to others, and making space for your own needs. Time boundaries prevent overextension and burnout.

- **Material boundaries** protect your money, possessions, and resources. They involve decisions about lending, sharing, and spending. Material boundaries prevent financial exploitation and maintain your independence.

I want you to be so good at taking care of yourself that you naturally gravitate toward reciprocal relationships in which you and your people can abundantly depend on each other. This starts with learning to establish clear, consistent boundaries:

- **Start small:** Pay attention to the subtle signs your body sends when something feels wrong: that knot in your stomach, that tension in your shoulders, that voice in your head saying, "This doesn't feel right." These signals tell you where you need boundaries.

- **Speak plainly:** Replace hints and hopes with clear statements. Instead of hoping someone will notice you're overwhelmed, say, "I need time alone to recharge." Instead of silently resenting extra work, say, "I can't take on more projects right now." Your needs deserve clear expression.

- **Stay firm but flexible:** Good boundaries bend when appropriate but don't break under pressure. You can adjust your plans for a true emergency while still protecting your regular need for rest. You might help a friend through a crisis while maintaining limits on how much you can give.

- **Practice makes progress:** Each time you honor your own limits, you build trust with yourself. Each time you express a boundary clearly, you teach others how to respect you. Each time you maintain a boundary despite pushback, you prove to yourself that your needs matter.

Celebrating Small Victories

When was the last time you celebrated yourself for having done so well and come so far? Not the big moments that everyone sees— the promotion, the degree, the milestone birthday. I mean the quiet victories that only you know about: eating dinner without checking your phone for the narcissist's messages, sleeping through the night without having any nightmares, making a decision without asking anyone else's opinion.

These small wins matter. Each time you trust your judgment, speak up in a meeting, or set a boundary, you're rebuilding the neural pathways that were damaged by abuse. Each time you choose yourself, you're proving that your old survival skills can become new strengths.

Victory isn't just about the finish line. It's about every step that got you there—even the stumbles, even the steps backward, even the times you had to stop and catch your breath.

Here's a list of small things you can do to show yourself what an absolute warrior you are for making it through another day:

- Mark your calendar when you notice moments of growth: the first time you fell asleep without checking the doors twice, the morning you enjoyed your coffee without rushing, or the day you wore that outfit they said "wasn't right" for you.

- Create rituals around your progress. Light a candle when you make it through a tough meeting. Take a victory lap around your block when you say no to something that doesn't serve you. Buy yourself flowers when you catch yourself trusting your own memory instead of doubting it.

- Keep a victory box. Drop notes in it every time you choose yourself: when you speak up in a meeting, when you set a boundary, when you make a decision without second-guessing it. On hard days, read through these notes and remind yourself of how far you've come.

- Build celebration into your daily routine. Take a moment each night to name one thing you did well, one step forward, or one moment of courage. Let yourself feel proud of these victories, no matter how small they might seem to others.

You are here; you are here in this body that carries you. In this body that breathes and lives and does for you, even when you doubt its strength. In this mind that protected you, that found ways to survive when survival seemed impossible.

You are here despite every voice that tried to convince you that you were too much or not enough. Despite every person who tried to shrink you, shame you, or silence you. Despite your own doubts and fears.

You are here, learning to trust yourself again, celebrate your victories, honor your boundaries, and speak your truth. Learning that resilience isn't about never falling—it's about knowing you can get back up.

And you will keep rising, keep growing, and keep healing. Not because someone else demands it, but because you choose it. Because you deserve it. Because you're worth every step of this journey back to yourself.

Chapter 5

Establishing Healthy Boundaries

This was an actual conversation between my ex-husband and me:

"That therapist is turning you against me," he said one night after I returned from a session.

"He's just helping me understand myself better," I replied.

"He's manipulating you. Filling your head with ideas."

"My healing journey is my business."

"I saw him too, remember? He's not good at his job. That's why I quit."

"He helps me, and I'm going to continue."

He couldn't make me stop therapy directly. So, he found my soft spot—our daughter. Suddenly, she was saying things like, "Dad says that therapist is making you think bad things about us." My heart broke hearing those words from her. We'd always been so close, and now he was using her as his proxy.

I almost gave in. Almost canceled my next appointment. Then I realized what was happening: He was using the person I loved the most to maintain control when his direct attempts had failed.

Setting boundaries after years of having them trampled feels like speaking a foreign language. But I found the words: "I love you both, but my therapy is my decision." My heart pounded saying it. My voice shook. But with each boundary I set, my voice grew stronger.

The change happens slowly, then all at once. One day, you realize you're no longer asking permission to have needs. You're no longer apologizing for taking up space. You're no longer explaining your right to privacy, to peace, to protection. You're simply claiming it.

This chapter isn't just about learning what boundaries are; it's about reclaiming your right to have them. It's about understanding that your limits aren't up for debate, your needs aren't negotiable, and your healing isn't someone else's property to control.

Recognizing Boundary Violations

How do you know that a boundary of yours has been violated? Easy: You'll feel so small, disgusted, and somehow guilty, as if you've done something wrong by simply existing with needs and limits. Your body will tell you before your mind catches up.

Maybe your shoulders creep up toward your ears. Maybe your stomach twists into knots. Maybe you find yourself holding your breath, making yourself quieter, trying to disappear. These physical reactions aren't random; they're your body's alarm system telling you something isn't right.

I remember sitting at my kitchen table, watching my coffee go cold while my mother told me all about my sister's private struggles—information my sister hadn't chosen to share with me. My throat felt tight. My hands went cold. Every cell in my body screamed, "This is wrong," while my mind was still catching up, still making excuses, still trying to convince myself that family meant having no boundaries.

Learning to recognize boundary violations isn't just about spotting the obvious crashes through your limits. It's about tuning into the subtle signals and quiet alarms that tell you when someone is pushing past your edges, even if they're doing it with a smile.

Physical Boundary Violations

Physical boundary violations happen in both obvious and subtle ways. They range from unwanted hugs and someone standing too close to more serious invasions, like going through your personal belongings or entering your space without permission.

Common Physical Boundary Violations

- **Your personal space gets invaded:** Someone leans too close during conversations, corners you in tight spaces, or blocks your path. They might dismiss your discomfort with, "Why are you so sensitive?" or "I'm just being friendly."

- **Touch becomes a tool of control:** They grab your arm to make a point, "playfully" push or poke you, or force hugs when you're clearly uncomfortable. If you object, they might say, "It's just a hug" or "Don't be so cold."

- **Your private space gets violated:** They enter your room without knocking, go through your phone or mail, or rearrange your belongings without asking. They act as if they're entitled to your space and possessions—as if your right to privacy doesn't exist.

- **Your bodily autonomy gets questioned:** They comment on your appearance, criticize your clothes, or pressure you to change how you look. They might touch your hair, face, or body without permission, treating your body as public property.

These violations often start small but escalate over time as abusers test and push your limits to see what they can get away with.

Emotional Boundary Violations

It's interesting, and somewhat revealing, how emotional boundary violations occur. They often bypass our defenses and are disguised as affection, compassion, or a desire to assist. Phrases like "I'm sharing this because I care" can pave the way for criticism. The phrase "I'm concerned about you" can be misconstrued as permission to dictate your decisions. The notion that "family shares everything" is used as an excuse for invading your privacy.

Think about the last time someone made you feel guilty for having an emotion they didn't approve of, or when your joy was labeled as bragging, your sadness as manipulation, your anger as overreaction. That's what emotional boundary violations feel like—a constant reshaping of your emotional reality to fit someone else's needs.

Let me break down exactly how these violations work and why they're so damaging:

- **Emotional dumping:** Someone unloads their problems on you without checking if you have the capacity to handle them. They treat you like an emotional waste bin, expecting you to process their feelings while ignoring your own limits. Your time and energy become their unlimited resource for venting, crisis management, and constant support.

- **Guilt manipulation:** They wield guilt like a master craftsman uses tools, shaping your behavior through carefully crafted phrases: "After all I've done for you" or "If you really loved me, you would..." These statements trap you in a cycle of proving your care through compliance.

- **Emotional invalidation:** Your feelings are measured against their standards and dismissed if they don't match their reality. Joy becomes bragging, hurt becomes manipulation, anger becomes overreaction. They position themselves as the authority on how you should feel, gradually eroding your trust in your own emotional experience.

- **Forced intimacy:** They demand emotional closeness on
  their timeline, pushing past your comfort level with
  demands for immediate trust and complete transparency.
  Your need for emotional space gets labeled as rejection,
  your privacy as secretiveness, and your boundaries as walls.

Time Boundary Violations

I remember a time when my ex would call me just five minutes before my sessions while I was getting ready to teach a class. He would
also walk into the room while I was live-streaming a fitness class for
my clients, bringing up random things he needed, and I couldn't
say anything since I was live on camera.

Time boundary violations show up in these persistent ways, wearing down your right to manage your own schedule. They disguise
themselves as urgency, as need, as dedication to your relationships.
The message becomes clear: Your time isn't really yours. "Just five
minutes" turns into an hour. "I need you right now" means dropping everything you're doing. "Why are you always too busy for
me?" makes you feel guilty for having other commitments. Your
schedule becomes a battlefield where saying "no" feels like starting
a war.

These violations take specific forms, each designed to keep you constantly available:

- **Constant interruptions:** The narcissist creates emergencies
  that demand your immediate attention. Every call must be

answered, every text returned instantly. Your focus on other tasks becomes proof that you don't care enough.

- **Time manipulation:** They show up late but expect you to wait. They create last-minute plans and get angry when you can't accommodate them. Your time becomes flexible while theirs remains rigid.

- **Schedule sabotage:** Important deadlines, meetings, or events suddenly face competing demands. They plan things that conflict with your commitments, forcing you to choose between their wishes and your responsibilities.

Even now, you might still believe that you need to be accessible, available, and always ready to drop everything when someone claims to need you—that giving away your time somehow proves your worth, your loyalty, and your love. This stops today.

Protecting your time means learning new responses:

- **Set clear time limits:** Before any meeting or call, state up-front how much time you have. "I can talk for 30 minutes" sets a clear expectation. Stick to it. When the time's up, end the conversation firmly but politely.

- **Create buffer zones:** Build space between commitments. Your time to recharge isn't selfish; it's necessary. Turn off notifications during focused work. Let calls go to voicemail when you're resting. The world won't end if you're not instantly available.

- **Learn to say no without explaining:**" That doesn't work for me" will become your new favorite phrase. No justifications needed. No elaborate excuses. Your time is yours to allocate as you choose. Other people's poor planning isn't your emergency.

- **Trust your calendar:** If someone asks for your time, check your calendar before answering. Don't let guilt or pressure make you overcommit. If you've scheduled time for yourself, protect it as firmly as you would any other appointment.

Managing Expectations in Relationships

One thing that I wish I'd known sooner (or, more accurately, at a younger age) is that our partners aren't really designed to complete us; rather, they're there to complement us. I think that where the wires usually get crossed is that we grow up hearing messages like "You'll find your other half" or "They'll make you whole"—as if we're somehow incomplete on our own.

These messages set us up for unrealistic expectations in relationships. We enter partnerships believing another person should fill our empty spaces, heal our wounds, and meet our every need. When they fail at these impossible tasks, we blame ourselves or think we made the wrong choice.

The truth is messier and more liberating: Healthy relationships happen between two whole people who choose to share their lives, not two half-people trying to become whole through each other. Each person brings their own strengths, weaknesses, dreams, and needs to the table.

Defining Clear Roles

Each relationship in your life serves a different purpose. Your best friend isn't your therapist. Your partner isn't your parent. Your coworker isn't your confidant. When roles get blurred, boundaries get crossed.

Healthy relationships need clear roles with defined limits. Your partner might support you through hard times, but they shouldn't be your only emotional support. Your friends might offer advice, but they shouldn't direct your decisions. Your family might care deeply about your well-being, but they shouldn't control your choices.

Real clarity is discussing specific responsibilities:

- Who handles which household tasks?
- How do financial decisions get made?
- What does emotional support look like for each person?
- Where does individual space end and shared space begin?
- When and how can you ask for help or changes?

These conversations aren't one-and-done. Roles shift as circumstances change, as people grow, and as needs evolve. The key is keeping the dialogue open and honest.

Discussing Relationship Expectations

We all go into relationships wanting what we want, needing what we need, and carrying our own invisible rulebook of how things should work. Some of us need daily check-ins to feel secure. Others need space to breathe. Some of us express love through touch and words, others through actions and time. When these unspoken rules clash, confusion and hurt follow.

Think about your last relationship. Did you ever find yourself saying, "But I thought..." or "I assumed you would..." or "Isn't it obvious that...?" These moments reveal the gaps between your expectations and reality, between your rulebook and theirs.

Healthy relationships require you to bring these invisible rules into the light. Not to judge them, not to decide whose map is "right," but to understand where your paths merge and where they diverge.

Here's how to have these crucial conversations without them turning into battlegrounds:

- **Choose a calm moment, not during conflict:** Begin with your own feelings and needs. "I want to share what's important to me in our relationship" opens dialogue better than "You never meet my expectations."

- **Key areas to discuss:** Time together and apart—how much alone time each person needs, what quality time looks like, and how to balance independence with togetherness.

- **Communication styles:** When to talk about problems, how to handle disagreements, and what kinds of support each person prefers during tough times.

- **Future visions:** Where each person sees the relationship going, what goals you share, and which individual dreams need space to grow.

- **Boundaries and deal-breakers:** What each person considers non-negotiable, where flexibility exists, and how to respect each other's limits.

Flexibility and Adaptability

Boundaries aren't meant to be set in stone; they're allowed to change as you grow, as your circumstances shift, and as your needs evolve. What worked for you last year might not serve you today. The boundary that protected you during the early stages of healing might feel too rigid once you've grown stronger.

Think of boundaries like the settings on a thermostat, not like the walls of a fortress—you adjust them based on the situation, the relationship, and the level of trust earned. Maybe you start with stricter limits while building trust with someone new. As they prove reliable, you might choose to be more flexible. If they break trust, you adjust accordingly.

This flexibility is wisdom. It shows you're paying attention to your needs and responding to real experiences rather than operating from fear or rigid rules. You might loosen some boundaries as you heal and tighten others as you learn more about yourself.

Here's how to maintain flexible boundaries while staying strong:

- Pay attention to how different situations and people affect you. Notice when you feel tense versus relaxed, drained versus energized. Your body's signals will help you adjust your boundaries before resentment builds.

- Take time each month to review your boundaries. Ask yourself: "Which ones still serve their purpose? Which feel too tight or too loose? Which need adjusting based on new circumstances or relationships?"

- Not every relationship needs the same boundaries. Close friends might have more access to your time than acquaintances. Family might need firmer boundaries than colleagues. Trust your instincts about what feels right with each person.

- As you heal and strengthen, you might find that old boundaries no longer fit. Maybe you can handle more social interaction now. Maybe you're ready to share more of yourself. Or maybe you discover you need stronger limits in certain areas.

- When you adjust a boundary, communicate it clearly: "I'm changing how I handle work calls after hours" or "I'm ready to share more about my past with you now." This helps others adapt with you.

Protecting Your Emotional Energy

Emotional energy is your capacity to handle life's psychological and emotional demands. It fuels your ability to process feelings, deal with challenges, support others, and stay resilient under stress. Just like physical energy lets you run a marathon, emotional energy lets you navigate relationships, work through conflicts, and maintain your mental well-being.

Think of it as a real, measurable resource. You're spending this energy every time you do the following:

- manage someone else's feelings
- process difficult emotions
- deal with conflict
- make tough decisions
- support others through crisis

And, like any resource, it can be depleted. When your emotional energy runs low, you might notice some or all of these signs:

- difficulty concentrating
- feeling overwhelmed by small problems
- emotional numbness
- increased irritability
- exhaustion that sleep doesn't fix

Like any precious resource, you need to know where it's going, how it's being spent, and who has access to your reserves. After giving away your energy to people who drained you dry, you need to be selfish and guard the resource well. Below, I'll show you how to protect and manage your emotional energy without shutting yourself off from meaningful connections.

Identifying Emotional Drains

Most of us move through our days reacting to emotional drains without really seeing them. We feel exhausted, but we can't pinpoint why. We know certain people leave us feeling empty, but we can't explain exactly how it happens. It's time to get specific—to name what drains you so you can guard against it:

- **Track your energy levels throughout the day:** Keep a simple log for one week. After each interaction or activity, rate your energy from 1 to 10. Note what happened, who was involved, and how you felt afterward. Patterns will emerge showing you exactly what and who drains you.
- **Watch for these common energy drains:**
  - people who always have a crisis that needs your immediate attention
  - conversations that leave you feeling confused about your own feelings
  - situations where you find yourself managing others' emotions
  - relationships where you give constant reassurance but receive none
  - activities that require you to suppress your true feelings

- **Notice your physical responses:**
  - a heavy feeling in your chest during certain conversations
  - tension headaches after spending time with specific people
  - tight shoulders when checking messages from someone
  - knots in your stomach before certain meetings or calls
- **Take action:** For each drain you identify, ask yourself:
  - "Does this person or situation need to be in my life?"
  - "Can I limit my exposure?"
  - "What boundaries would help protect my energy here?"
  - "How can I respond differently to reduce the drain?"

Keep this energy log for at least two weeks. Look for patterns. Which people consistently appear on days when your energy drops? What types of interactions leave you feeling depleted? This information will be your guide for setting new boundaries and protecting your emotional energy.

Creating an Emotional Safe Space

I read something the other day about soft landing places. It talked about how birds always know where to rest their wings—how they instinctively find branches that will hold them when they're tired of flying. Humans need these landing places too: spaces where we can rest without our guard up and where we can set down the weight of always being alert.

You can't create an emotionally safe space until you understand what makes you feel secure, protected, and at peace. It's about building an environment where your body can relax, your mind can be quiet, and your spirit can breathe. Like those birds finding their perfect branch, these experiences teach you to be on the lookout for the things that support you and the things that don't.

We all deserve to have a soft place to land. If you don't have one, I'll show you how you can create one for yourself:

- Pick your spot—a window seat, the end of your couch, or an unused corner in your bedroom. Make it yours with specific touches that ground you: your grandmother's quilt, that wind chime from the beach trip where you first felt free, the mug that fits perfectly in your hands.

- The first hour shapes your whole day. Guard it like gold. Maybe you read one poem with your coffee. Maybe you sit in your garden and listen to the birds waking up. Maybe you write three pages of whatever crosses your mind, no editing allowed.

- When day turns to night, signal to your brain that it's safe to power down. Light a candle that smells like pine forests. Put on music that reminds you of rain. Wrap yourself in something soft. Let your shoulders drop. Let your jaw unclench.

Reinforcing Boundaries Consistently

Your boundaries will be resisted by some, but that doesn't necessarily mean they're wrong. In fact, the people who push back hardest against your boundaries are often the ones who benefited most from you not having any. Their resistance proves your boundaries are working.

Think about a garden fence. Its job isn't to look pretty; it's to protect what grows inside. The rabbits who used to feast freely on your vegetables won't like it. The neighbors who liked to cut across your yard won't understand why they suddenly can't do so anymore. But the fence stands anyway, doing its job without apology.

Your boundaries work in the same way. Each time you hold them, despite pressure to give in, you strengthen them. Each time you stay firm, even when someone calls you selfish or difficult, you prove to yourself that your limits matter.

When Boundaries Get Tested

Every time you state a boundary then let it slide, you teach people that your "no" can become a "yes" with enough pressure. Like a parent who says "absolutely not" then caves after enough whining, inconsistent boundaries invite testing and pushback. They signal that your limits are negotiable if someone tries hard enough.

Consistency builds trust—not just with others, but with yourself. When you maintain your boundaries reliably, you prove to yourself that you mean what you say. Your word becomes your bond, your limits become real, and your self-respect grows stronger.

Here's what happens when boundaries get pushed:

- **Direct challenges:** Someone might openly question or dismiss your boundary: "You're being too sensitive" or "That's ridiculous." Stand firm. Repeat your boundary calmly without defending or explaining it.

- **Guilt trips:** Watch for manipulation through guilt: "After everything I've done for you" or "I guess I'm just a terrible person then." Recognize these as attempts to make you abandon your limits.

- **Testing and probing:** Some people will try small violations to see what you'll allow: a scheduled call that runs "just five minutes" over, or a personal question that pushes past your comfort zone. Address these immediately—small breaches will grow into big ones.

When your boundary gets challenged, your first instinct will likely be to explain, defend, or even apologize for it. Don't do that; instead, use what therapists call the "broken record" technique. Repeat your boundary in simple, clear terms: "I don't discuss my finances." If they push, say it again. No elaboration needed.

For the persistent boundary pushers, distance is your best tool. When someone repeatedly ignores your "no calls after 9 p.m." boundary, let their calls go to voicemail. When they complain, simply state: "As I mentioned, I don't take calls after 9 p.m. You can reach me tomorrow." Their reaction to your boundary is their business, not yours.

Watch for the sneaky boundary erosion—the "just this once" requests that try to create exceptions. Remember, each exception becomes someone's evidence that your boundary is flexible. That colleague who keeps pushing work discussions into your lunch break? "I'm not available for work talk during lunch" should be your mantra, even if you're just scrolling on your phone.

Power plays often follow boundary setting. Someone might try to punish you with silence, exclude you from events, or spread rumors about how you've "changed." This is information—it shows you exactly who benefited from your previous lack of boundaries. Let their reaction strengthen your resolve, not weaken it.

There's an expression that says that if you can't stand your own company, you'll accept anyone into your life. And isn't that true, and humbling to a certain extent? When we don't feel whole on our own, we let people cross lines that shouldn't be crossed, accept behavior that shouldn't be accepted, and stay in situations that drain our spirit.

But here's what changes when you learn to value your own company: You start to recognize that boundaries aren't just about keeping others out; they're about creating space for yourself to grow. You begin to understand that being "difficult" or "too sensitive" is

often just someone else's response to you valuing yourself enough
to say no.

The work of boundaries is really the work of coming home to yourself. Of learning that you're worth protecting. Of understanding
that your space, your time, and your energy are precious parts of
you that deserve to be guarded with care.

Chapter 6

Cultivating Emotional Well-Being

What does it even mean to process emotions? To me, it felt like adopting a victim mentality, and I refused to enter that space. On one side, I moved through life pretending I wasn't feeling anything, because acknowledging my feelings would mean confronting a lot of pain. On the other side, when things seemed good, I felt like I could be pulled under at any moment. It was akin to ignoring that I was walking on a tightrope and, at any moment, I could fall to either side.

Learning to navigate emotions takes time. It requires patience with yourself and an understanding that feelings are like weather patterns moving through your internal landscape. They shift and change shape. Sometimes, they gather into storms; sometimes, they break into unexpected moments of clarity. Always, they carry messages about what matters to us, what hurts us, and what we need to heal.

The Role of Creativity in Healing

Creative expression activates different parts of your brain than logical thinking or speech. When you engage in creative activities—
whether it's painting, writing, music, or movement—you access
emotional experiences stored in your body and brain that you might
not be able to reach through talking alone.

During creative activities, your brain releases dopamine and sero-
tonin, chemicals that help regulate mood and reduce stress. This
physiological response helps calm your nervous system, making it
easier to process difficult emotions without becoming overwhelmed.

Creating something gives you tangible control over your environment. You decide which colors to use, which words to write, and
which shapes to form. This sense of agency helps rebuild confidence
and decision-making abilities that may have been damaged.

Creative expression provides a container for complex emotions. Instead of trying to explain or understand your feelings logically, you
can pour them into a song, a painting, or a dance. This external rep-
resentation helps create distance between you and overwhelming
emotions, making them easier to process.

Through creativity, you develop new neural pathways in your brain.
Each time you express yourself creatively, you're literally building
new connections that your brain uses to process your emotions.

Here are four great practices you can use for healing:

- **Writing/journaling:** Beyond basic diary keeping, therapeutic writing involves specific techniques. Stream-of-consciousness writing lets you pour out thoughts without censoring or editing. Writing letters you'll never send helps you express difficult feelings safely. Writing poetry allows you to find metaphors for experiences that feel too raw to approach directly. The key is writing without judgment—no editing, and no worrying about grammar or structure.

- **Making visual art:** This includes drawing, painting, or sculpting without focusing on your skill level or the end result. Use color to express emotions you can't put into words. Create abstract shapes to represent feelings or experiences. The physical act of making marks or molding materials engages both your body and your mind in processing experiences. The focus needs to stay on the process of creating rather than producing "good" art.

- **Movement and dance:** Moving your body freely helps you release trauma and emotions stored in your muscle memory. This isn't about choreographed dance but about authentic movement, letting your body express what it needs to express. You might move slowly or quickly, gracefully or jaggedly. The goal is following your body's impulses rather than planning your movements.

- **Music and sound:** This includes both making and listening to music. Drumming helps release anger and anxiety through rhythm. Humming or singing specific sounds can help regulate your nervous system. Even creating playlists that match or shift your emotional state can be therapeutic. The vibrations and rhythms of music affect your body at a physiological level and support you to integrate your experiences in different ways.

Managing Triggers and Anxiety

Our triggers show us all the places where we still need to heal— where we're sensitive and most likely to react rather than respond. They point to wounds that haven't fully closed, to memories our bodies still carry, and to stories we haven't fully processed yet.

Think of the last time something triggered you—maybe it was a tone of voice, a specific phrase, a scent, or even a seemingly inno-cent situation. Your heart raced. Your palms got sweaty. Maybe your mind went blank or was flooded with memories. Your body responded before your mind could catch up, activating old survival patterns you thought you'd left behind.

These reactions aren't signs of weakness or proof that you're "too sensitive." They're your nervous system doing exactly what it's learned to do to keep you safe. The problem isn't that you have trig-gers—it's that no one ever taught you how to work with them, how to understand their messages, and how to respond instead of react.

What Are Triggers?

Triggers are intense emotional and physical reactions activated by specific situations, words, or experiences that remind your brain and body of past trauma. When triggered, your nervous system responds as if the original threat is happening again, launching you into a fight, flight, or freeze response.

Common triggers include:

- specific words or phrases the abuser used
- certain tones of voice or facial expressions
- feeling trapped or unable to leave a situation
- someone standing too close or touching you without permission
- being criticized or questioned
- having your perception doubted
- sudden loud noises or unexpected changes
- feeling ignored or dismissed

Physical responses to triggers include:

- racing heart
- shallow breathing
- muscle tension
- sweating
- nausea
- dizziness

- feeling frozen
- difficulty focusing

Emotional responses include :

- sudden anxiety or panic
- intense anger
- overwhelming sadness
- feeling disconnected from reality
- facing thoughts
- confusion
- shame
- fear

Grounding Techniques

Grounding is a way to bring yourself back to truth and reality when your mind pulls you into panic, fear, or disconnection. It's taking the time to anchor yourself in the present moment when triggered memories or anxiety try to drag you into the past or future.

What makes grounding effective is that it gives your brain concrete, immediate data from your surroundings. When you're triggered, your brain can't tell the difference between past and present danger. Grounding techniques help your brain recognize where you are right now, in this moment, where you're actually safe.

Here are some specific grounding techniques that will help you re-connect to the present.

The 5-4-3-2-1 Technique

This mindfulness practice brings your awareness to your senses, connecting you to the here and now:

1. Take a deep breath and check your inner climate. Notice how you feel inside. Refrain from judging what you find as good or bad.

2. Leaving your eyes open, look at your environment and notice five things you can see. With each of the five items, pause and observe.

3. Notice four things you can feel in your body—for example, the contact of your clothes with your body, your hair brushing against your skin, the contact point between your body and the chair, your feet touching the ground. Rest your attention on each sensation for a few deep breaths.

4. Name three things you can hear. Try to choose three different sounds, near and far, such as the sound of a car, the hum of the fridge, or even an internal sound, like your stomach rumbling.

5. Note two things you can smell. It can be something in the environment, or maybe the laundry detergent in your clothes and the shampoo in your hair.

6. Finally, explore one thing you can taste. It may be the leftover taste of a meal, your toothpaste, or just your breath.

Continue using the five senses to connect with the present moment as you go through your day.

Physical Grounding

Try the following practices to physically ground yourself in the present:

- If possible, remove your shoes and socks and press your feet firmly into the ground. Feel the sensation of the earth beneath your feet. There's no need to think about anything; just stay present with the sensations of the ground beneath your feet. You're here, now; you're safe and secure.

- Hold an ice cube or run water over your hands, feeling the sensation of coolness or warmth on your hand.

- Hold an object in your hands. If you're outdoors, choose something natural (a stone or a flower, or place your hand on a tree trunk); if you're indoors, you can place your hand on any object, like a chair, your coffee mug, or a pen. Feel its textures, weight, and temperature.

In the beginning, my grounding object was a book (the one I was meant to buy all along), which I carried everywhere. One day, I saw a friend struggling, and I gave the book to her. At that moment, I realized how far I'd come; it was almost like a rite of passage. Find a meaningful object to carry with you—something that can serve as a grounding symbol. It could be a small stone, a piece of jewelry, or even a book that holds significance for you.

Mental Grounding

When your mind spins with intrusive thoughts or memories, these mental grounding techniques create anchors for your attention.

They work by engaging the logical part of your brain, gently pulling you away from emotional flooding and back to the present moment. These exercises require just enough focus to interrupt anxious patterns without feeling overwhelming:

- Name all the states or countries you know.
- Count backward from 100 in 7s.
- Describe your surroundings in detail.
- Name items in categories (e.g., types of dogs, colors, cities).

Creating a Trigger Management Plan

You'll likely recognize this pattern: You scour the internet for answers and diagnose yourself through strangers' posts, falling down research rabbit holes at 2 a.m. We look for certainty in medical websites and forums, hoping to find the perfect explanation that will make everything make sense. But these digital journeys often leave us more anxious and more confused, with a head full of worst-case scenarios.

In my case, while still married, I began to experience a variety of symptoms in my body. Doctors couldn't find anything wrong with me, so I started looking for answers online regarding a possible disease. I quickly realized that I would begin to exhibit all the symptoms I read about, which would trigger a panic attack. Therefore, I stopped reading medical articles. That's when I realized I needed more than just coping skills; I needed a clear, written plan I could follow even when my mind went blank.

What works better than endless searching is creating something solid to hold on to—a personalized plan that grounds you when panic hits, when memories flood in, and when your mind can't find its way back to safety.

This plan isn't just about surviving triggers; it's about learning to navigate them with increasing confidence. Each time you use your plan, you reinforce the message to your brain and body that you can handle these moments, that you have tools, that you're not helpless anymore.

This is exactly how to create a trigger management plan for yourself, step by step.

Step 1: Identify Your Triggers

Keep a detailed log for two weeks. Note:

- what triggered you:

  _____

  _____

  _____

- where you were:

  _____

  _____

  _____

- what happened just before:

_____

_____

_____

- your physical and emotional reactions:

_____

_____

_____

- how intense the reaction was (on a scale of 1–10):

_____

_____

_____

Step 2: Map Your Warning Signs

Document your personal signs of escalating stress:

- early warning (tension in shoulders, irritability)
- mid-range (heart racing, difficulty focusing)
- crisis point (panic, dissociation)

Step 3: List Your Specific Responses

Create three levels of response:

- mild trigger response (deep breathing, walking)
- moderate trigger response (calling a friend, grounding exercises)
- severe trigger response (contacting therapist, calling a crisis hotline)

Step 4: Build Your Support System

Create a contact list:

- primary support person
- backup support person
- professional help (therapist, counselor)
- crisis resources

Step 5: Develop Your Safety Protocol

Write out specific steps for severe triggers:

- where to go
- who to call
- what to say
- what you need

Developing Emotional Intelligence

Our ability to be in life is directly connected to our ability to feel what we're feeling in the moment and to accept that what we're feeling is valid. For years during and after narcissistic relationships, many of us learned to doubt our emotions and question whether we had the right to feel hurt, angry, or afraid.

Emotional intelligence is the ability to understand what our emotions are telling us and responding to them with wisdom instead of reaction. When we feel anger, it might be telling us about crossed boundaries. When we feel fear, it might be warning us about genuine danger or echoing old wounds.

It takes a lot of trial and error—and time—to learn to read these emotional signals. It requires us to sit with feelings we've been taught to ignore or suppress. It means trusting that our emotional responses, even when they're uncomfortable, carry important messages about our needs, our boundaries, and our healing.

Identifying Emotions

Language and expression are a very big part of healing work. Without the right words to name what we're feeling, emotions can feel like a tangled mess inside us. Think about the difference between saying, "I feel bad" and being able to say, "I feel disappointed because my trust was betrayed" or "I feel anxious because this situation reminds me of past manipulation."

When we can name our emotions precisely, we gain power over them. They become experiences we can understand rather than overwhelming forces that control us. This isn't about analyzing every feeling to death; it's about developing a richer emotional vocabulary that helps us make sense of our inner world.

Many of us have a limited emotional vocabulary because we were taught to suppress or deny certain feelings. Anger was labeled as "too aggressive." Sadness was seen as "weakness." Fear was dismissed as "being too sensitive." Learning to identify and name our emotions means unlearning these judgments.

This is how you can expand your emotional vocabulary and learn to read your own emotional signals more clearly.

Primary vs. Secondary Emotions

Primary emotions are our first, instinctive responses to a situation. They rise quickly and pass through us if we let them flow. But often, we've learned to cover these primary emotions with more "acceptable" secondary emotions. Here's how this layering works.

Primary emotions might be:

- hurt when someone dismisses your feelings
- fear when someone raises their voice
- grief when you lose a connection
- joy when you accomplish something

But instead of feeling these directly, you might experience secondary emotions:

- anger instead of hurt (because anger feels more powerful than pain)
- numbness instead of fear (because fear feels too vulnerable)
- irritability instead of grief (because grief feels too overwhelming)
- self-doubt instead of joy (because you were taught to minimize your successes)

To unravel these layers, you have to dig beyond the surface and ask questions:

- When you're snapping at everyone, ask yourself: "Am I actually scared about something?"
- When you can't stop cleaning, ask yourself: "What feelings am I trying to control?"
- When you're criticizing yourself, ask yourself: "What hurt am I trying to protect myself from?"

Body–Emotion Connection
Your body emotes long before your mind can put words to feelings. Each emotion creates distinct physical sensations; this is your body's emotional map.

When anxiety rises, it might show up as:

- butterflies or knots in your stomach
- shallow breathing in your chest
- tingling in your hands and feet
- tension across your shoulders

- a racing heart or pulse

Anger often appears through:

- a tight, clenched jaw
- hands balling into fists
- heat rising in your face and neck
- pressure building in your head
- energy surging through your arms

Sadness tends to manifest as:

- heaviness in your chest
- your throat feeling tight or constricted
- your shoulders curving inward
- your limbs feeling heavy or weak
- your eyes filling with tears

Joy expresses itself through:

- warmth spreading through your chest
- the muscles relaxing in your face
- energy flowing freely through your body
- your breathing becoming deeper and easier
- your shoulders dropping away from your ears

These physical signals will help you catch emotions early, before they overwhelm you. Your body always tells the truth about what you're feeling; it's just a matter of learning to listen.

Expanding Your Emotional Vocabulary

When you say, "I'm angry," you're capturing just one shade of a complex emotion. Anger has many faces:

- frustration when obstacles block your path
- irritation as a result of small annoyances that are piling up
- rage when boundaries get violated
- indignance when facing injustice
- resentfulness when feeling taken for granted

When you say, "I'm sad," you're simplifying a deep emotional experience:

- disappointment when expectations aren't met
- grief for what you've lost or never had
- loneliness during disconnection
- melancholy when remembering the past
- heartbreak when trust gets betrayed

When you say, "I'm happy," you're summarizing various positive states:

- contentment in peace
- excitement about new possibilities
- peacefulness when feeling safe
- satisfaction after accomplishment
- joy during genuine connection

Daily Emotion Check-Ins

Choose specific times each day, such as in the morning, at noon, and in the evening, to pause and ask yourself:

- "What am I feeling in this moment?"
- "Where do these emotions live in my body?"
- "What triggered these feelings?"
- "What do these emotions need from me right now?"

Remembering Empathy

Every now and then, we need to specifically remind ourselves that empathy includes self-empathy as well—that the compassion we so readily offer to others deserves to flow back to ourselves. Empathy might be about understanding others' pain, but it's also about honoring our own experiences. When we judge ourselves for not healing faster, for having bad days, or for still feeling angry or hurt, we're denying ourselves the very understanding we'd offer a friend in our situation.

Remember: You're not just the survivor of your story; you're also the one who needs to hear that survival was brave. You're not just the one who endured; you're also the one who needs gentleness as you heal. Being empathetic with yourself means acknowledging that your feelings matter, your experiences were real, and your healing deserves patience.

Chapter 7

Fostering Connections
and Community

I can't remember when I last had a table full of joyful, kind, and happy people around me. That's a thought I had about three months before I decided that I was leaving him. The realization hit me while I was washing dishes, staring out of the kitchen window at my neighbor's house where people came and went freely, where laughter drifted across the fence, and where life seemed to flow without permission or apology.

My world had shrunk so gradually that I'd hardly noticed it happening. First, friends stopped calling because I always had to cancel. Then family visits became shorter because the tension was too thick. Even casual conversations with neighbors dwindled because I'd learned to hurry from car to door, avoiding any chance of social connection that might trigger questions or criticism later.

Seeking Supportive Communities

Isolation doesn't happen overnight. It happens in small surrenders, declined invitations, shortened conversations, and avoided social gatherings. Each tiny retreat feels like choosing peace or avoiding conflict—until, one day, you find yourself alone, standing at a kitchen window, watching other people live while your own life stays on pause.

A healthy community offers more than just social connection. It provides mirrors that reflect your true self back to you, not the distorted image the narcissist created. These are people who validate your experiences without keeping you stuck in them—who understand why certain things might trigger you but don't treat you as if you're fragile.

The right community includes people at different stages of healing. Those who've walked the path before you can show you what's possible. Others who are on similar journeys can share their current struggles and victories. Even people who haven't experienced abuse directly but who bring genuine empathy and understanding add valuable perspective to your support network.

Online vs. Offline Communities

There are many different ways to reach out and connect with others who understand your journey. Some find comfort in the glow of a screen, sharing their story with people across the world who are awake at 3 a.m. when sleep won't come. Others need the warmth of human presence and the reassuring touch of a hand on their shoulder in a support group meeting.

Both online and offline communities serve vital roles in healing, each offering unique advantages. Your choice might depend on where you are in your journey, what feels safe right now, and what kind of support you need most.

Online Communities

These spaces offer immediate connection from the safety of your home. Support groups, forums, and social media communities focused on healing let you connect with others who share similar experiences worldwide. You can participate at your own pace, choose your level of involvement, and maintain privacy while still sharing your story.

The digital world also provides access to resources and perspectives you might not find locally. You can learn from others' experiences, share insights, and find validation any time of day. Many people find it easier to open up about difficult experiences when typing rather than when speaking face to face.

Offline Communities

In-person connections offer something screens can't replicate: the healing power of physical presence. Local support groups, workshops, or even informal meetups provide opportunities for real-time interaction and deeper relationship building. Body language, tone of voice, and shared physical space create different levels of understanding and support.

Face-to-face communities also help you practice social skills and boundary setting in real life. They provide opportunities to rebuild trust gradually through consistent, in-person interactions.

The strongest support networks often combine both online and offline connections. Each serves different needs at different stages of healing. Online communities might feel safer when you're first reaching out, while in-person connections may become more important as you rebuild trust in relationships.

Sharing Your Story Responsibly

Sharing your story of survival and healing can be a powerful part of recovery. When done thoughtfully, telling others about your experience helps you process trauma, validates your journey, and connects you with others who understand. It can transform private pain into shared strength and wisdom.

But sharing requires careful consideration. Your story isn't just a collection of events; it's your lived experience, your emotional truth, your personal journey. How, when, and with whom you share affects both your healing and your safety. Some people might dismiss or minimize your experience. Others might use your vulnerability in harmful ways. Even well-meaning listeners might offer unwanted advice or comparisons that do more harm than good.

Responsible sharing means choosing spaces and people who can hold your story with respect and understanding. This might be a therapist trained in trauma work, a support group for survivors, or close friends who've proven their trustworthiness. These safe spaces allow you to speak your truth without fear of judgment, unsolicited advice, or breaches of confidence.

Importance of Boundaries When Sharing

Setting boundaries around your story isn't selfish—it's essential. When we share our experiences of abuse and survival, we make ourselves vulnerable. While this vulnerability can create powerful connections, it also requires protection. Think of your story as something precious that you choose to share, not something others have the right to demand.

Boundaries around sharing take many forms. Sometimes, it's about choosing which details to keep private. Other times, it's about deciding when and where you'll discuss your experiences. Often, it's about recognizing who has earned the right to hear your story and who hasn't.

Let me explain exactly how to set these boundaries:

- When someone asks about your experience, have clear responses ready. This isn't about being rude or defensive; it's about maintaining healthy limits. You might say, "I appreciate your interest, but I only discuss certain aspects of my story" or "I'm willing to share the general outline, but some details need to remain private."
- Watch for people who try to push past these limits. They might press for more details after you've set a boundary or

share your story with others without permission. Some people compare their experiences in ways that minimize yours or try to explain away abusive behavior. These are signs that they're not ready to hold your story with respect.

- Remember that you can change your mind at any time. Maybe you started sharing and realize it feels too vulnerable. Perhaps the conversation is heading into territory you're not ready to discuss. It's okay to say, "I need to stop here" or "Let's talk about something else now." Your comfort and safety come first.

- Handle intrusive questions with simple, firm responses: "That's not something I discuss." "I'll let you know if I want to share more." "Let's focus on the present rather than the past."

Your story belongs to you. You decide how much to share, when to share it, and with whom. This isn't about keeping secrets—it's about honoring your journey and protecting your peace.

Using Your Story to Inspire

When we share, we give other people who've experienced the same things permission to speak their truth too. Your story might be the key that unlocks someone else's silence, the light that shows them they're not alone, or the mirror that helps them recognize their own experience.

This doesn't mean you have to become a public speaker or write a book. Sometimes, the most powerful sharing happens in quiet moments: a gentle word to someone who's struggling, a knowing look that says "I understand," a simple "me too" that bridges the gap between isolation and connection.

Your journey of survival and healing, shared at the right time with the right people, will become part of a larger communal experience of recovery. Each story shared helps break the silence in which abuse thrives, creates ripples of understanding, and shows others that healing is possible—that they too can find their way back to themselves.

Participating in Group Therapy

It was uncomfortable at first, I won't lie. Sitting in that circle of folding chairs, clutching my coffee cup like a shield, listening to strangers share pieces of their lives that mirrored my own. I kept thinking I was in the wrong place, that my story wasn't "bad enough," that these people would think I was making a big deal out of nothing.

Then Sarah spoke about how her ex would always check her phone, "just because he cared so much." How he'd question every text, every call, every interaction. My coffee cup froze halfway to my lips. That was my story too. Then Mike talked about walking on eggshells, about never knowing which version of his partner he'd face each day. My hands started shaking. That was my life too.

When that first session came to an end, my coffee was cold and untouched, but something inside me had warmed up. These people got it. They understood the subtle manipulation, the crazy-making doubts, the slow erosion of self. Nobody questioned whether it was "bad enough." Nobody told me to just get over it. For the first time, I didn't have to explain or justify or defend my experience.

How to Find the Right Therapist and Group

Not all groups are created equal. Some focus solely on sharing stories, others on specific healing techniques. Some welcome anyone who identifies as a survivor, while others might be gender-specific or focus on particular types of relationships. Finding the right fit matters because this space will become part of your healing journey.

When searching for a therapy group, consider both the practical and emotional elements. The group's structure should feel contained but not rigid. A good leader will explain how they run sessions, handle triggering situations, and maintain boundaries. They should be able to tell you about their specific experience with recovery from narcissistic abuse and their approach to group dynamics.

Watch for how the leader manages the group's energy. Do they ensure everyone gets a chance to speak? Can they gently redirect someone who's dominating the conversation? Do they know how to ground the group when emotions are running high? These skills make the difference between a helpful therapeutic space and one that might retraumatize you.

Pay attention to your comfort level with the group's size and format. Some people feel overwhelmed in larger groups, while others find smaller groups too intense. Some might prefer a women-only space, while others feel comfortable in mixed groups. Consider practical factors too: location, timing, cost, and commitment requirements.

Most importantly, trust your instincts. If something feels off about a group, even if you can't explain why, listen to that feeling. You might need to visit several groups before finding the right fit. That's normal and part of the process of honoring your needs.

Participation Dynamics

Participation dynamics refers to how people interact and engage within a therapy group. If you walked into a room where eight people were seated in a circle, you'd notice that some would be leaning forward to listen, while others would be eager to share. Others would be sinking back into their chairs, arms crossed; one person might be dominating the conversation while another hasn't spoken in three sessions.

A typical group session might flow like this: Sarah shares her struggle with setting boundaries with her ex. Two people nod in recognition. James jumps in to give advice, while Maria sits quietly, tears in her eyes. The facilitator notices Maria's reaction and creates space for her to share if she wants to.

These interactions create patterns. Some people process out loud, sharing every thought. Others absorb silently, processing internally.

Some react emotionally to others' stories. Others intellectualize everything to keep their emotions at bay.

The group becomes a microcosm of real-world relationships. Old patterns start to reappear: people-pleasing, caretaking, withdrawing, controlling. But here, in the safety of the group, you can notice these patterns and practice new ways of engaging.

Here are some tips on how to successfully navigate a group setting:

- **Be mindful of your patterns:** Notice how you naturally behave in the group. Do you jump in to fix others' problems? Shrink into silence? Share every detail? Compare your struggles to others'? Understanding your default mode helps you make conscious choices about how you participate.

- **Find your pace:** Share gradually. Start with smaller, less emotionally charged pieces of your story, watch how the group responds, and notice how you feel afterward. This helps you build trust with the group while honoring your own comfort level.

- **Practice active listening:** When others share, resist the urge to prepare your response. Instead, really listen. Notice their body language, their tone of voice, and the emotions beneath their words. This deepens your capacity for connection and helps you learn from others' experiences.

- **Manage your triggers:** Sometimes, others' stories will hit close to home. You might feel overwhelmed or angry, or you may want to shut down. Use these moments to practice self-regulation. Take deep breaths. Ground yourself by feeling your feet on the floor. If needed, signal to the facilitator that you need a break.

- **Have boundaries:** It's okay to say, "I'm not ready to talk about that yet" or "I need to step back today." Learn to recognize and express your limits. Watch how stating your boundaries clearly and calmly feels different from withdrawing or building walls.

- **Show up authentically:** When you do share, speak from your own experience. Use "I" statements. Share your feelings and needs rather than giving advice. This helps create safety for others while deepening your own healing work.

The Impact of Trust in Groups

It may be hard to imagine yourself in a group setting, opening up to people you've barely ever said a word to—people who were strangers just weeks or months ago. Opening your mouth to share pieces of your story might feel like standing on the edge of a cliff: Your heart races, your palms sweat, and your mind screams that it's not safe to be this vulnerable.

I remember sitting in my first group session, listening to others share their stories. Each time someone spoke about their experience, another person would nod in recognition or wipe away tears. Slowly, I realized something powerful was happening. These weren't just strangers anymore; they were witnesses to each other's truth. No one rushed to fix or judge. They just held space and offered understanding.

Something shifts when you sit in a circle of people who get it, who don't need you to explain why you stayed, why you doubted yourself, why you're still struggling to trust. The silence after someone shares isn't empty—it's full of recognition, of shared understanding, of collective healing.

Benefits of Peer Mentorship

When I was walking through a shopping center a few weeks back, I ran into someone from my support group. Two years ago, she sat where you sit now: shaking, uncertain, full of doubt. Today, she has this quiet strength about her. Over coffee, she told me how strange it felt to now be the one offering hope to newcomers in the group, when not long ago she couldn't imagine feeling whole again.

That's the power of peer mentorship. It's not just about having someone give you advice or share their story. It's about seeing living, breathing proof that you can move through this darkness and find light again. It's about learning from someone who knows exactly why you check your phone 50 times before sending a text or why you apologize for needing anything.

Here's what makes peer mentorship so powerful:

- **Shared experience:** Your mentor understands the subtle manipulation tactics you've faced because they've faced them too. They get why certain situations trigger anxiety, why trust feels impossible, and why you doubt your own judgment. This deep understanding creates a unique kind of safety.

- **Practical wisdom:** They can share specific strategies that worked for them—how they rebuilt boundaries, recognized red flags, learned to trust their instincts again. These aren't textbook solutions but real-world tools tested by experience.
- **Living proof:** Seeing someone who's further along in their healing journey provides tangible hope. Their progress shows you what's possible, while their ongoing work shows you that healing isn't about reaching perfection.

How to Find a Mentor

Finding a mentor isn't like scrolling through dating profiles or hiring an employee. It's about recognizing someone whose healing journey resonates with your own, someone whose growth gives you hope. Often, these connections develop naturally in support groups or recovery communities.

Look for someone who:

- has moved beyond simply surviving to actually thriving
- speaks about their experience with wisdom rather than fresh pain
- shows humility about their own ongoing healing
- respects boundaries and demonstrates emotional stability
- listens more than they advise
- shares insights without trying to control your journey

Start by:

- participating actively in support groups
- attending workshops or recovery programs
- joining online communities focused on healing
- noticing who consistently offers balanced, hopeful perspectives
- watching how potential mentors interact with others

The right mentor won't try to fix you or make you follow their exact path. They'll share their experience while honoring your unique journey and celebrate your progress without making it about them. Most importantly, they'll understand that healing isn't linear and won't expect perfection.

Becoming a Mentor

There will come a point when you realize your story could help light the way for someone else—not because you've figured everything out, but because you remember exactly how that darkness feels. You know the weight of self-doubt, the fog of confusion, and the fear that you'll never feel whole again.

Becoming a mentor is teaching yourself to hold space for someone else's healing while continuing your own. It's about sharing your hard-won wisdom without trying to force someone down your exact path. Each time you help someone spot a red flag you missed or trust an instinct they're doubting, you strengthen your own healing too.

This role carries sacred responsibility. You're not there to rescue or fix anyone. You're there to walk beside them, sharing what you've learned, celebrating their progress, and reminding them of their strength when they forget. Each person you support will help you understand your own journey more deeply, seeing new layers of growth you hadn't recognized before.

This is what you can do to effectively honor their journey and hold space for yours as well:

- While your experience matters, resist the urge to turn every conversation back to your story. Listen deeply to understand their unique situation. Share your insights only when relevant—and always in ways that emphasize their power to choose their path.

- Set specific times for contact. Be clear about what support you can and cannot offer. Remember, you're not their therapist, crisis counselor, or savior. Guide them toward professional help when needed.

- Instead of saying, "You should..." or "You need to...," try "Here's what helped me..." or "Something to consider is..." Let them find their own way, even if it's different from your path.

- Continue your own healing work. Stay in therapy if needed, and maintain your own boundaries and self-care practices. The stronger your foundation, the better you can support others without depleting yourself.

- Some will take your advice, others won't. Some will move quickly, others slowly. Your role isn't to push or pull, but to witness and support their unique path to healing.

The Power of Vulnerability in Community

We learn a lot as we grow older, as we have things happen to us, and as we try and try again. I mean, think about it: We come into this world completely open, trusting, willing to share every joy and hurt. Then life teaches us to build walls, to guard our hearts, and to keep our pain private. By the time we reach adulthood, we've mastered the art of "I'm fine" even when we're breaking inside.

But here's what life has taught me lately: Those walls that once protected us can become our prisons. In my support group, I watched a woman share how she still sleeps with the lights on. Another admitted she checks her door locks five times each night. Someone else confessed they haven't dated in three years. With each honest admission, the room felt lighter, as if we were all setting down heavy bags we'd been carrying alone.

Something powerful happens when we stop pretending we've got it all figured out—when we can say, "I'm struggling" or "I'm scared" and hear others say, "Me too." It's like finding your way home after being lost for so long, this feeling of finally being seen—truly seen, not just the polished version we show the world but all of our messy, beautiful truth.

What Is Vulnerability?

If I share something with you that's usually difficult for me to express—something like, "Oh, today was hard. Despite how far I've come, how happy and content I'm becoming, I really miss him"—it's an attempt at vulnerability. It's choosing to share a truth that feels risky, that exposes the parts of ourselves we usually keep hidden.

Vulnerability is opening ourselves to being truly seen, wounds and all. It's admitting we don't have all the answers, that we're still figuring things out, and that healing isn't linear. It means sharing not just our triumphs but also our doubts, our fears, our seemingly contradictory feelings.

This kind of honest sharing creates real connection because it touches the universal human experience of struggle and uncertainty. When we drop the mask of having it all together, when we share what's real instead of what's comfortable, we create space for authentic healing.

Discernment is needed for vulnerability because you don't necessarily need to share everything with everyone; you must be selective and be honest only with those people who've proven themselves trustworthy. This then means learning to recognize the difference between sharing to connect and sharing to offload, between opening up to heal and opening up to hurt ourselves again.

Practicing healthy vulnerability is like learning a new language—
one where you speak the truth instead of deflect. So, trust your gut
about when to share, because vulnerability often comes in whispers,
in admitting you're not okay when everyone expects you to be fine;
on other occasions, it roars, aligning with your throat chakra and
giving you the tenacity to stand in a group and finally say out loud
the truth you've been choking on for years.

Look out for the spaces that feel like oxygen instead of drowning.
Places where your words are met with quiet understanding rather
than rushed advice. People who can sit with your pain without trying to sweep it away with toxic positivity or quick fixes.

Learn the difference between sharing from a place of self-trust versus one of self-doubt. Real vulnerability doesn't ask for validation
or permission to feel what you feel. It doesn't come with an apology
attached. It simply says: "This is my truth, this is where I am, this is
what's real for me right now."

Move at your own pace. There's no rush. There'll be times when
you want to share deeply and other days when you might need to
pull back and process privately. Both are valid; both are part of your
truth and part of the experience of learning to trust yourself and
others again.

I know that you're trying, that you're a person who wants to cup joy
in their hands and show up tenaciously for each day, for yourself,
and for your healing. I see how hard you're working to trust again,

to share your truth, to let others in even when every instinct is screaming at you to keep your walls up.

Your willingness to be vulnerable, to let yourself be seen—including all the messy, imperfect, beautifully human bits—is remarkable. Each time you share your story, someone else in the circle feels less alone. Each time you admit to struggling, you give someone else permission to be honest about their struggles too. So, keep showing up, in whatever way feels right today. Whether that's speaking your truth out loud or simply holding space for others to share theirs, you're helping to build the kind of community we all needed when we were lost in the dark.

Chapter 8

Thriving Beyond Survival

It's Friday, just like any other Friday, and I've just bought myself a new dress. I'm twirling in the fitting room feeling like a giddy five-year-old again, and all feels right in the world. The dress is strapless, in bright summer colors that catches the light. My ex used to always buy me black—not the sexy kind, but the kind you'd wear to a funeral. This dress has flowers on it—big, bold, and bright, seeming to dance with every spin. For a moment, I catch my reflection mid-twirl and freeze. Not because anything's wrong, but because everything feels so wonderfully right.

Three years ago, I wouldn't have even tried this dress on. "Too bright," he'd say. "Not age-appropriate." I'd put it back and choose something beige or black—something safe that wouldn't make waves. But today, in this fitting room mirror, I see a woman who lights up at sunflowers, who twirls just to hear the fabric swish, who buys what makes her heart sing.

The saleswoman knocks to check if I need another size. "I'm perfect," I call out, and my hearts softens ever so slightly when I realize that I mean what I say and say what I mean. I'm not perfect as in flawless, but perfect as in whole, perfect like myself. I can hear the melody of hangers sliding on racks and some distant chatter from outside the fitting room, and my own happy humming is jovially filling the gaps in the space where criticism used to reside.

In that moment, surrounded by discarded clothing options and the gentle buzz of fluorescent lights, I remember all the times when I made myself smaller, duller, less. How I'd learned to shop quickly and efficiently, choosing clothes that wouldn't "cause problems." Now I take my time. I try things on just because they catch my eye. I buy colors that match my joy instead of his approval.

The dress is draped over my arm when I walk to the register, and as I take one foot and place it in front of another, I can't help but think how I get it now. I get what Audre Lorde meant when she wrote, "When I dare to be powerful, to use my strength in the service of my vision, then it becomes less and less important whether I am afraid" (Lorde, n.d.).

Defining Personal Success and Fulfillment

Funny how time changes things, isn't it? Three years ago, "success" was simply making it through dinner without being criticized for my cooking, dodging debates on historical events, or having my laugh—after just one glass of wine—pointed out as if I'd done something wrong,

Now, success looks different. Sometimes it's as simple as buying groceries and only buying what I want to eat. Sometimes it's sleeping through the night without checking the locks twice. Sometimes it's looking in the mirror and actually holding my own gaze, seeing myself instead of searching for flaws he would have pointed out.

Yesterday (well, the day before I started writing this chapter), I was humming while cooking dinner. Just me in my kitchen, dancing freely between the stove and the counter, adding spices without measuring, tasting as I went. No one to please but myself. No one to apologize to. Just the simple joy of making a meal I wanted to eat, in a kitchen that felt like mine, in a life that finally felt like it belonged to me. How freeing. How lovely. How wholesome.

Personal Values

Personal values are your core beliefs about what's important in life; they shape what you prioritize, what you stand for, and what you won't compromise on. Think of them as your non-negotiables, the lines you won't cross even when pressured.

These lines usually get a little blurry after we've been through traumatic experiences, so rebuilding clear values will help you trust yourself again. When you know deep down that honesty matters to you, you'll recognize instantly when someone is asking you to lie. When you value respect, you'll feel the discord immediately if someone treats you poorly.

Your values are also decision-making tools that will help you decide if you should you stay in that friendship where you're always walking on eggshells, or if you should maintain contact with someone who repeatedly crosses your boundaries. The clarity that comes from doing this protects you from falling back into situations that harm your spirit. You won't need to agonize over every choice or seek others' approval. You'll know in your bones what fits with who you are and what doesn't.

I want to help you now to identify your core values through self-reflection. Here are key values many people connect with:

- **authenticity:** being true to yourself
- **courage:** facing challenges with strength
- **compassion:** showing kindness to others and yourself
- **growth:** learning and evolving
- **independence:** making your own choices
- **integrity:** doing what's right even when it's difficult
- **peace:** maintaining inner calm
- **connection:** building genuine relationships
- **creativity:** expressing yourself freely
- **security:** feeling safe and stable

Now ask yourself:

- "When do I feel most alive and true to myself?"
- "What makes me feel proud of my choices?"
- "What situations make me feel uncomfortable or wrong?"

- "What do I want people to remember about me?"
- "What would I stand up for, even if I stood alone?"
- "When did I last feel deeply satisfied versus times I felt ashamed?"

Your answers will guide you toward times when your core values are either honored or violated.

For example:

- If hiding your opinions makes you feel sick inside, authenticity might be a core value.
- If rushing past someone in need haunts you, compassion might be key.
- If letting others make your choices feels wrong, independence matters deeply to you.

Setting Standards

You're allowed to have standards, you're allowed to have things that you will and will not tolerate, and you're allowed to raise those standards as you grow. Setting standards protects your peace, your healing, your right to be treated with respect.

From every relationship that hurt you, you learned something valuable about what you need. You learned to recognize red flags—the subtle signs that someone won't respect your boundaries. You learned to trust that knot in your stomach when someone crosses a line. These lessons shape your standards now.

Your standards are the foundation of healthier relationships. They help you recognize people who will treat you with respect, who will honor your boundaries, who will add peace to your life rather than chaos. They guide you toward connections that lift you up rather than wear you down.

This is how you set and enforce standards:

1. **Draw wisdom from your past:** Each difficult experience taught you something. The partner who criticized your appearance showed you the importance of acceptance. The friend who shared your secrets taught you about trust. Use these lessons to shape what you'll accept now.

2. **Name your standards clearly:**
   o "I need honesty in my relationships, even when the truth is uncomfortable."
   o "I expect my feelings to be heard and respected, not dismissed or mocked."
   o "I want relationships where both people take responsibility for their actions."

3. **Back your standards with action:**
   o Address it directly the first time.
   o Set a clear consequence if it happens again.
   o Follow through if the behavior continues.

4. **Listen to your intuition:** Pay attention when something feels wrong. That unease usually means one of your standards has been crossed. Don't talk yourself out of your feelings or make excuses for others' behavior.

Remember and remind yourself of this as many times as you need to: Your standards aren't threats or ultimatums but rather clear expressions of how you need to be treated to feel safe and respected. You don't need to justify or defend them.

Creating a Success Statement

I watched a lot of motivational talks. I still love to watch them, and when I do, I'm very deliberate about paying attention to the speakers' choice of words. I notice how they frame success, how they build their story arc, how they intertwine their triumphs and failures into something meaningful.

One speaker's words stuck with me. She talked about writing her own success statement, which wasn't some generic "I want to be happy and rich" declaration but a real, raw vision of what success meant to her after years of feeling like her luck in life had run dry. Her success, as she defined it, was being able to wake up each morning and being able to recognize herself in the mirror again. About making decisions without second-guessing every choice. About laughing freely without monitoring her volume.

That night, I sat down and wrote my own success statement. Not what success should look like according to social media or self-help books, but what it meant to me, now, after everything. What would make me feel like I was truly living, not just surviving?

What Is a Success Statement?

A success statement captures your personal vision of thriving, not just surviving. It's deeper than goals like "get a promotion" or "buy a house." It's about who you want to be, how you want to feel, and what kind of life you want to create for yourself.

Your success statement needs to reflect your truth, not someone else's expectations. Think about moments when you feel most alive, most yourself. Maybe success means falling asleep without checking the locks three times. Maybe it's expressing an opinion without apologizing. Maybe it's choosing what to cook for dinner without hearing that critical voice in your head.

Here's how to draft your statement:

1. Start with "I am..." and write about who you're becoming, not just what you're doing. For example:
   o "I am someone who trusts her own judgment."
   o "I am creating a life where peace is normal, not a luxury."
   o "I am building relationships where I can be fully myself."
2. Add specific feelings and experiences you want:
   o "I wake up looking forward to my day."
   o "I make decisions without seeking approval."
   o "I express my needs without fear."

Let your statement evolve as you grow. What felt like success six months ago might be just your starting point now. That's not moving the goalposts; that's expanding your vision of what's possible for your life.

Setting New Life Goals

The beauty of starting over again is that you'll get to experience the joy of having many firsts again. Firsts like eating at a restaurant and ordering exactly what you want, not what someone else thinks you should have. Firsts like decorating a room in colors that make your heart sing wildly out loud, not colors that won't "cause problems." Firsts like going to bed when you're tired and waking up when your body is ready.

These seem like small things to someone who's never had their choices controlled. But for those of us who have, these are revolutionary acts of rebellion. Each one represents a piece of ourselves we're taking back, a freedom we're relearning to enjoy.

I remember my first solo grocery shopping trip after leaving. I stood in the ice cream aisle for about 20 minutes because I was so overwhelmed by the choices, and because I'd realized that I could buy the "sugary" ice cream he always said was so bad for you. I had tears in my eyes right there between Ben and Jerry's Cherry Garcia and Häagen-Dazs Double Belgian Chocolate Chip, not because I was sad but from the simple joy of having the freedom and space to choose something *just because I wanted it.*

SMART Goals Framework

Okay, you're not rebuilding one part of your life but your entire world. This isn't just about career goals or financial targets—it's about reconstructing every aspect of who you are and how you live.

Think of it as creating a new blueprint for your life, one that includes everything from how you spend your Sunday mornings to how you handle workplace conflicts.

SMART goals take on a deeper meaning when you're rebuilding your life. Yes, they should be Specific, Measurable, Achievable, Relevant, and Time-bound, but they also need to honor your healing journey. Let's break this down:

- **Specific:** Instead of "Be happier," define exactly what happiness looks like in your new life. Maybe it's "Create a morning routine that starts my day with peace" or "Establish three new friendships where I can be myself."

- **Measurable:** Track your progress in ways that matter to you, not just as numbers on a page. Count the days you speak up in meetings, the times you make decisions without second-guessing, the moments you choose your own needs over others' demands.

- **Achievable:** Start where you are, not where you think you "should" be. If walking into a crowded restaurant alone feels impossible right now, begin with ordering takeout from a new place. Build your confidence in steps.

- **Relevant:** Every goal should align with your values and support your healing. Ask yourself: "Does this goal come from my true desires or from old programming about what I 'should' want?"

- **Time-bound:** Give yourself realistic time frames that account for the natural ebb and flow of healing. Some weeks, you'll leap forward; others, you'll need to rest and regroup.

Let's look at how this framework applies to different areas of life.

Personal Growth

Personal growth is you getting to rediscover who you were before someone tried to reshape you. It's about taking back the voice that was silenced, the dreams that were dismissed, and the parts of yourself you had to hide away. Start with specific steps that build your trust in yourself. Rather than vague aims like "be more confident," set specific markers:

- Speak up in three team meetings this month.
- Make one decision daily without seeking approval.
- Try one new activity every month that scares me a little.

Relationships

Building a healthy support network means being intentional about who you let into your life and how you show up in relationships. It means creating connections where you can be authentic, where your boundaries are respected, and where you feel seen rather than scrutinized. Consider these concrete steps toward healthier relationships:

- Attend two social events monthly where I might meet like-minded people.

- Practice setting one boundary each week in existing relationships.
- Spend 30 minutes daily nurturing connections that make me feel strong.

Health and Well-Being

For many of us, "getting healthy" turned into another way to try to please others or another source of shame when we couldn't meet impossible standards. After living with someone who might have criticized your body, controlled your food choices, or dismissed your health concerns, reclaiming your physical well-being is a deeply personal act of self-care. This isn't about crash diets or punishing exercise regimes. It's about learning to listen to your body again, to honor its needs, to treat it with the kindness it deserves after everything it's carried you through. Start with small, concrete steps. For example, instead of "get healthy," define what that means for you:

- Schedule my long-delayed medical checkups by the end of this month.
- Learn three new recipes that nourish my body and soul this week.
- Create a bedtime routine that helps me feel safe and peaceful.

Lastly, here are ten things I want you to remember. Ten gentle reminders that I can only hope will be a soft landing place for you:

- Buy the bright yellow dress. Wear the red lipstick. Order the spicy food. Take up space.
- That playlist he said was "too emotional"? Play it loud. Dance in your kitchen.
- When the old voice in your head says "you can't," remember how many times you already have.
- Your home doesn't need to be Instagram-perfect; it just needs to be yours.
- That thing you want to try but think you're too old for? Do it anyway.
- The friends who stuck around? They're your family now. The ones who left? They made space for better ones.
- Keep that box of memories if you want to. Look at it when you need to remember how far you've come.
- Those "irrational" fears? They kept you alive. Thank them, then let them rest.
- Paint your walls. Change your hair. Move your furniture. Make your space yours again.
- That wild, messy laugh you were told was "too much"? Someone's waiting to laugh with you.

Embracing a Growth Mindset

The heart and brain like to hold on to what's familiar, what feels safe, even though it might not necessarily be the healthiest thing for us. Like how we keep checking our ex's social media even though it hurts, or hesitate to try new things because the old ways, painful as they were, feel more predictable.

Our minds create these well-worn paths, like trails through a forest that we follow without thinking. We know exactly where the rocks and roots are, exactly how to navigate the darkness. The idea of cutting a new path feels overwhelming, dangerous even. What if we get lost? What if the new way is worse?

But growth means being willing to step off those familiar trails. It means understanding that just because something is comfortable doesn't mean it's good for us. Just because we know how to survive in toxic situations doesn't mean we have to keep practicing those survival skills.

Growth vs. Fixed Mindset

A growth mindset believes that our abilities, intelligence, and qualities can be developed through effort, learning, and persistence. This perspective sees challenges as opportunities to grow, mistakes as chances to learn, and setbacks as temporary obstacles rather than permanent failures.

In contrast, a fixed mindset views our traits as static and unchangeable. It assumes our abilities are carved in stone—that we're either naturally good at something or we're not. This mindset leads us to avoid challenges for fear of failure, give up easily when facing obstacles, and see effort as fruitless.

These mindsets shape how we approach healing and recovery. Someone with a growth mindset understands that their past experiences shaped them but don't define them. They believe they can learn new ways of relating, develop stronger boundaries, and build healthier relationships through conscious effort and practice.

However, someone with a fixed mindset might think, *I'll always be damaged* or *I'll never trust again*. They see their trauma responses as permanent rather than patterns that can be understood and gradually changed. This mindset can keep them trapped in cycles of victimhood and hopelessness.

The key difference lies in how each mindset interprets challenges. A growth mindset sees difficulty as a sign of learning and stretching beyond comfort zones, while a fixed mindset interprets struggle as proof of inadequacy or failure. One empowers change while the other reinforces limitation.

Accepting Criticism

Accepting criticism, not as a personal attack but as a tool for learning, takes practice, especially when in the past it was used as a weapon to control or to diminish you. After experiencing narcissistic abuse, any feedback might feel like an echo of those old wounds, triggering defensive responses or self-doubt.

Learning to distinguish healthy criticism from manipulation means understanding the key differences between them. Constructive feedback focuses on specific behaviors, not your character. It offers suggestions for improvement rather than blanket condemnation. It comes from a place of support, not control. Most importantly, it respects your right to accept or decline the feedback.

When criticism is healthy, you'll notice that it feels different in your body too. Instead of having that familiar knot of shame in your stomach or the urge to defend yourself, you'll feel curious, thoughtful, or even energized by the possibility of growth. You can disagree without fear of punishment. You can take what serves you and leave what doesn't.

The goal isn't to become immune to feedback or to accept every criticism as truth. Instead, it's about developing the discernment to recognize the feedback that helps you grow while maintaining firm boundaries against judgments that seek to diminish you. It's about trusting yourself to know the difference.

Ways to Hold Criticism With Grace

- **Listen, then react:** When receiving feedback, pause before responding. Notice your physical reactions, such as a racing heart, a tightening of your shoulders, and defensive thoughts. These reactions often come from old wounds, not the present moment. Take a breath. Create space between the feedback and your response.
- **Ask questions that clarify:**
  o Could you give me a specific example?
  o What would you suggest I do differently?
  o How would that approach work better?

These questions help you understand if the feedback is actually constructive and useful.

- **Evaluate the source and intent:** Think about whether this person has the expertise to offer this feedback. Do they have your best interests in mind? Are they critiquing something you can actually change? Are they offering solutions or just pointing out flaws?

- **Separate the content from the delivery:** Sometimes, valuable feedback is delivered clumsily. Learn to extract useful insights even when the presentation isn't perfect. Focus on what you can learn rather than how it was said.

- **Process and take time to reflect on feedback before deciding what to do with it:** Ask yourself:
  - "Does this feedback align with my values and goals?"
  - "Will making this change serve my growth?"
  - "Is this something I want to work on, or am I doing it to please others?"

Celebrating Freedom and Independence

This is a journal entry I made a couple of months ago:

Freedom is a word that has been coming up a great deal of times lately. So I guess today, I'll write about what freedom has felt like lately...

Freedom is making plans without checking with anyone first; the spontaneity in deciding to take a different route home because the sunset looks particularly beautiful. Last night, I even left dirty dishes in the sink until morning and, spoiler alert, the world didn't end.

I caught myself turning up the heat when I felt cold, without calculating if I deserved the extra expense. I watched true crime documentaries on Netflix, the ones he said were "too dark." Let my phone ring three times before answering, my heart steady, my breath calm.

I even rearranged my entire living room at midnight just because I felt like it. I pushed furniture around in my pajamas, making scratching sounds on the floor that would have once earned me hours of silent treatment. I hung art on walls without measuring twice, without worrying if the holes would make someone angry. When I finished, I sat in my imperfectly arranged room and felt something unfamiliar—peace.

Today, freedom tastes like ordering spicy food without hearing comments about my "sensitive stomach." It sounds like my full-throated laugh echoing through open windows. It feels like wearing red lipstick to the grocery store, taking up space, letting myself be seen.

Freedom lives in the space between choosing myself, trusting myself, being myself, and aligning my spirit with the things that make me smile, make me dance, and make me feel alive and lucky to be me.

Maybe these things aren't a big deal, or maybe they're just about everything. Maybe they're proof that I'm no longer surviving but actually living. Maybe they show how far I've come from the woman who used to ask permission to exist. And maybe, just maybe, that's the biggest victory of all: the fact that I'm not leaving or running but that I'm allowing myself to just.... be.

Recognizing Freedom

I can't define freedom for you; that's something you'll have to do by yourself, and your definition will likely change as you heal, as you grow, as you rediscover who you are without someone else's voice in your head.

For some, freedom starts with small acts of reclaiming control— choosing what to eat, when to sleep, how to spend a Sunday afternoon. For others, it shows up in bigger moments—traveling alone, speaking up in meetings, dating again. There's no universal road map, no checklist of what freedom should look like.

Your journey to freedom might look messy. You might take two steps forward, one step back. You might find yourself suddenly overwhelmed by choices you never had before. You might discover that on some days, freedom feels scary; after all, you spent years being told what to do, how to feel, who to be.

Take time to explore what freedom means to you now. Notice when you feel most like yourself, when your shoulders relax, when your breath comes easily. Pay attention to moments when you catch yourself smiling for no reason or making a choice without second-guessing it. These moments are showing you what your freedom looks like.

Independence

I've come to love my independence. I love that I can do things for myself, by myself. But in that space where I've grown to be content with doing things alone, I recognize that it's also okay to have days when I want someone by my side. Days when I wish I had a hand to hold while walking through the farmers' market or someone to share that sunset with.

Independence isn't about being an island. It's not about proving I can do everything alone. Some mornings, making my own coffee feels like victory. Other mornings, I miss the simple act of making coffee for two. Both feelings can exist at once.

I've learned that true independence means having the strength to stand alone and the wisdom to know when to let others in. It means fixing my own leaky faucet with YouTube tutorials, and also know-ing it's okay to call a plumber when I need to. It means being whole on my own while still leaving room for connection.

This balance looks different for everyone. Maybe it's learning to en-joy solo dinners at restaurants while also accepting invitations to group gatherings. Perhaps it's taking pride in managing your finances independently while being open to discussing money matters with trusted friends. It could be cherishing your solitary morning routine while acknowledging that sometimes you'd like to share breakfast with someone special.

The key is understanding that needing others doesn't negate your independence. You can be fiercely self-reliant and still want companionship. You can celebrate your ability to handle life's challenges alone while remaining open to support. You can protect your hard-won independence while creating space for healthy interdependence. This is how you do it:

- **Create your independence map:** Some days demand solitude—those quiet morning hours with just coffee and silence. Other days call for connection, for shared laughter over breakfast, for someone to witness your life. Learning to honor both needs without guilt or justification is part of reclaiming your independence. Pay attention to what each day asks of you.

- **Keep what's special:** Certain moments belong to you alone. Maybe it's Sunday afternoons exploring the city, reading in parks, discovering new coffee shops. These aren't just activities; they're declarations of independence. When others ask to join, you get to decide. Your "yes" or "no" doesn't need an explanation or apology.

- **Share from a place of choice:** Think about the difference between helping someone because you want to and doing so because you feel you must. True independence lets you choose connection without needing it to prove your worth. Notice how different it feels to offer support from a place of strength rather than obligation.

- **Move in sync with the waves:** Independence isn't a straight line. Some days, it feels like freedom, like power, like possibility. Other days, the weight of handling everything alone feels heavy. Both experiences shape your journey. Let them teach you about what you need, what you want, and what you're capable of.

- **Build bridges, not walls:** You don't have to isolate yourself or refuse help. You can choose when and how to connect with others. You have the liberty to say, "I can manage this alone, but I'd welcome your company" without feeling like it diminishes your strength.

Creating Rituals for Celebration

Certain moments feel like an "I love you" to life, with life saying it right back at you. Like when you catch the first cherry blossom of spring floating down exactly as you walk beneath the tree or find that perfect song on the radio just when you needed to hear it. These aren't coincidences; they're reminders that you're exactly where you need to be.

The universe has its own way of celebrating your freedom. It shows up in sudden bursts of laughter that bubble up from nowhere, in the satisfaction of making your own choices, and in the peace of falling asleep in clean sheets that smell exactly the way you like them. And yes, in the sunrise that appears to remind you that you've made it to yet another beautiful day.

When you finally let yourself live out loud, life starts living back. It's in the warmth of the sun on your face during a midday walk you chose to take. It's in the taste of the food you ordered spicy because that's how you actually like it. It's in every small moment that reminds you that you're not just existing anymore—you're alive.

How to Live Out Loud

I can't tell you how to find these moments—they're different for everyone. But they hide in the most unexpected places. Like last night, when a summer storm rolled in and, instead of rushing inside, I stood on my porch watching lightning split the sky. The air felt electric, alive, and for a moment I was purely present, purely free.

These moments sneak up in quiet ways too. Like waking up before your alarm and realizing you can watch the sunrise simply because you want to. Or cooking a complicated recipe just for yourself, taking three hours to make something beautiful just because it brings you joy. Not for Instagram, not for anyone else—just for you.

Sometimes, they explode into your day—like when your favorite song comes on and you find yourself dancing in your kitchen, wooden spoon as a microphone, singing at the top of your lungs. Or when you're driving down an empty road with your windows down, wind in your hair, no destination in mind, just the pure pleasure of movement and freedom.

This is how you LOL—or, as I sometimes say, how you "live out loud":

- **In relationships:** It means expressing your needs without first calculating if you've earned the right to have them. It's saying, "I don't like that" without adding, "but it's okay" to soften the blow. It's letting people see your messy moments, your wild dreams, your raw emotions—not to get attention, but because authenticity is no longer negotiable.

- **In daily life:** It shows up in decisions both big and small. Ordering what you actually want at restaurants instead of what's easiest. Wearing the outfit that makes you feel alive instead of the one that helps you blend in. Dancing in your living room not because no one's watching but because you no longer care if they are.

- **In your space:** Your home becomes a reflection of your unleashed self. Maybe that means painting walls in colors that make your heart sing, creating a meditation corner even though someone once called it "woo-woo," or leaving your art supplies out because your creativity doesn't need to hide anymore.

- **At work:** It appears in speaking up during meetings without monitoring your tone. In pursuing projects that excite you instead of just playing it safe. In setting boundaries around your time and energy without feeling guilty.

I've learned that no one can be excited for you, and no one can celebrate things for you. At the end of the day, it's all a matter of how you choose to mark your own moments of triumph. Here's how you can celebrate your victories, both the big and small ones:

- Buy yourself flowers not because something special happened, but because you made it through another week standing tall.

- Write yourself love notes. Leave them in places you'll find later—your coat pocket, your desk drawer, between the pages of your journal.

- Take yourself on dates. That new café you've been curious about? Don't wait for company. Go alone, order your favorite drink, and toast to your own company.

- Document your wins. Take photos of moments that make you proud—the first meal you cooked in your new kitchen, the wall you painted yourself, the morning you woke up feeling peaceful.

- Create rituals that honor your progress. Light a candle each time you set a boundary. Take a victory lap around your block when you speak your truth. Buy a new book when you survive a hard week.

- Mark your calendar with private celebrations, such as the day you left, the day you found your own place, or the first time you slept through the night without checking the locks.

Each small goal you set, each boundary you maintain, each moment you choose yourself adds up to something powerful: a life lived on your own terms, in your full voice, without apology or permission. This is what it means to truly break the chains.

Conclusion

So, here we are at the end of this book, but maybe at the starting point of your healing journey. Can you still remember how I told you about that night I spent on my couch sobbing while my now ex-husband slept soundly upstairs? Now I sleep in a bed that's entirely mine, in a home where my laughter bounces off walls that have never heard anyone tell me to be quiet.

The fog I described at the start of this book, that disorienting haze of self-doubt and confusion—it lifts. Not all at once, not like a curtain being pulled back, but slowly, like dawn breaking. One day, you realize you've made a decision without second-guessing yourself. Another day, you catch your reflection and actually smile at what you see.

That guide I promised you? It's not just this book. It's your own inner wisdom waking up again. It's your body remembering how to trust its signals. It's your heart learning to beat to its own rhythm instead of someone else's demands.

You're not the same person who started reading these pages, just like I'm not the same person who sat in that therapist's office trying to find what was wrong with me. We're both learning to write new stories, to trust our own truth, to believe in the clarity that comes after the confusion.

Take what you need from these pages. Your path won't look exactly like mine, but that's the point. You're not following someone else's map anymore. You're creating your own.

Review Request

If this book resonated with you, I'd be truly grateful if you could take a moment to leave a review on Amazon. Your reviews help other women—those still seeking answers and healing—discover this book when they need it most. Even a few words can make a big difference. Thank you for reading, for your healing journey, and for being part of this story.

With gratitude,

Autumn B. Hayes

References

American Psychiatric Association. (2022). *Diagnostic and statistical manual of mental disorders* (5th ed., text rev.). American Psychiatric Publishing.

Adams, A. E., Sullivan, C. M., Bybee, D., & Greeson, M. R. (2008). Development of the Scale of Economic Abuse. *Violence Against Women, 14*(5), 563–588. https://doi.org/10.1177/1077801208315529

Creswell, J. D. (2017). Mindfulness interventions. *Annual Review of Psychology, 68*, 491–516. https://doi.org/10.1146/annurev-psych-042716-051139

Dokkedahl, S. B., Kokshun, K., Kristiansen, J., Elklit, A., & Gondan, M. (2019). The psychological subtype of intimate partner violence and its health consequences: A systematic review. *Systematic Reviews, 8*, 113. https://doi.org/10.1186/s13643-019-1049-7

Dutton, D. G., & Painter, S. L. (1993). Emotional attachments in abusive relationships: A test of traumatic bonding theory. *Violence and Victims, 8*(2), 105–120.

Fincham, G. W., Strauss, C., Montero-Marin, J., & Cavanagh, K. (2023). Effect of breathwork on stress and mental health: A meta-analysis of randomised-controlled trials. *Scientific Reports, 13*, 432. https://doi.org/10.1038/s41598-022-27247-y

Hardesty, J. L., Crossman, K. A., Haselschwerdt, M. L., Johnson, M. P., & Raffaelli, M. (2015). Toward a standard approach to operationalizing coercive control and classifying violence types. *Journal of Marriage and Family, 77*(4), 833–843. https://doi.org/10.1111/jomf.12187

Johnson, M. P., & Kelly, J. B. (2008). Differentiation among types of intimate partner violence: Research update and implications for interventions. *Family Court Review, 46*(3), 476–499. https://doi.org/10.1111/j.1744-1617.2008.00215.x

Linehan, M. M. (2015). *DBT skills training manual* (2nd ed.). Guilford Press.

Miller, J. D., Lynam, D. R., Hyatt, C. S., & Campbell, W. K. (2017). Controversies in narcissism. *Annual Review of Clinical Psychology, 13*, 291–315. https://doi.org/10.1146/annurev-clinpsy-032816-045244

Neff, K. D., & Germer, C. K. (2013). A pilot study and randomized controlled trial of the Mindful Self-Compassion program. *Journal of Clinical Psychology, 69*(1), 28–44. https://doi.org/10.1002/jclp.21923

Pincus, A. L., & Lukowitsky, M. R. (2010). Pathological narcissism and narcissistic personality disorder. *Annual Review of Clinical Psychology, 6*, 421–446. https://doi.org/10.1146/annurev.clinpsy.121208.131215

Polusny, M. A., Erbes, C. R., Thuras, P., Moran, A., Lamberty, G. J., Collins, R. C., Rodman, J. L., Stahre, M. A., & Lim, K. O. (2015). Mindfulness-based stress reduction for posttraumatic stress disorder among veterans: A randomized clinical trial. *JAMA, 314*(5), 456–465. https://doi.org/10.1001/jama.2015.8361

Postmus, J. L., Stylianou, A., & McMahon, S. (2016). The Abusive Behavior Inventory–Revised and the Scale of Economic Abuse–12: Validation in diverse samples. *Journal of Interpersonal Violence, 31*(21), 3547–3572. https://doi.org/10.1177/0886260515585541

Prochaska, J. O., & DiClemente, C. C. (1992). Stages of change in the modification of problem behaviors. *American Psychologist, 47*(9), 1102–1114.

Schultz, K., Cattaneo, L. B., Sabina, C., Brunner, L., Jackson, S., & Serrata, J. V. (2016). Key roles of community connectedness in healing from trauma. *Psychology of Violence, 6*(1), 42–48. https://doi.org/10.1037/vio0000025

Southwick, S. M., Bonanno, G. A., Masten, A. S., Panter-Brick, C., & Yehuda, R. (2014). Resilience definitions, theory, and challenges: Interdisciplinary perspectives. *European Journal of*

Psychotraumatology, 5, 25338.
https://doi.org/10.3402/ejpt.v5.25338

Stark, E. (2007). *Coercive control: The entrapment of women in personal life.* Oxford University Press.

Tang, Y.-Y., Hölzel, B. K., & Posner, M. I. (2015). The neuroscience of mindfulness meditation. *Nature Reviews Neuroscience, 16*(4), 213–225. https://doi.org/10.1038/nrn3916

U.S. Department of Veterans Affairs & Department of Defense. (2023). *VA/DoD Clinical Practice Guideline for the Management of Posttraumatic Stress Disorder and Acute Stress Disorder* (Provider Summary).
https://www.healthquality.va.gov/guidelines/MH/ptsd/

White, S. J., Dillon, G., Butchart, A., & Garcia-Moreno, C. (2023). Intimate partner violence and mental health outcomes: A systematic review and meta-analysis. *Trauma, Violence, & Abuse.* https://doi.org/10.1177/15248380231158763

Zaccaro, A., Piarulli, A., Laurino, M., Garbella, E., Menicucci, D., Neri, B., & Gemignani, A. (2018). How breath-control can change your life: A systematic review on psychophysiological correlates of slow breathing. *Frontiers in Human Neuroscience, 12,* 353. https://doi.org/10.3389/fnhum.2018.00353

About the Author

Autumn B. Hayes is a meditation coach, spiritual mentor, and author whose spiritual awakening began in 2009. She helps women rebuild confidence, sharpen their intuition, and step into the healthiest, clearest versions of themselves—mentally, emotionally, and physically. A survivor of narcissistic relationships within her family and marriage, Autumn now guides others through a holistic blend of mindfulness, mindset coaching, and personal transformation.

As the creator of *Journey to Balance: 21 Days for Anxiety & Depression*, she teaches meditation to individuals, corporate teams, and spiritual seekers around the world. With over a decade of experience, her work bridges science and soul, offering foundational tools for beginners alongside deeper insight practices for advanced students.

Her work is for women who are done surviving and ready to move forward with purpose. Through meditations, writing rituals, healing programs, and wellness practices, Autumn supports her clients in creating peaceful minds, strong bodies, and lives fully aligned with who they are becoming.

Autumn lives in Tampa, Florida, where her mornings begin with coffee, a workout, and quiet time with her cat, Kiki.

Connect with Autumn:

TikTok: @mindfulnesswithautumn
Email: support@energiamindfulness.com
Website: www.energiamindfulness.com

If you'd like to deepen and expand the work you've started in this book, explore the Life After The Narcissist Companion Journal with all the prompts from this book, plus exclusive exercises and reflections only available in the journal. Available in paperback through Amazon and major booksellers.